The Governance of European Higher Education

Convergence or Divergence?

Bloomsbury Higher Education Research

Series Editor: Simon Marginson

The Bloomsbury Higher Education Research series provides the evidence-based academic output of the world's leading research centre on higher education, the ESRC/RE Centre for Global Higher Education (CGHE) in the UK. The core focus of CGHE's work and of The Bloomsbury Higher Education Research series is higher education, especially the future of higher education in the changing global landscape. The emergence of CGHE reflects the remarkable growth in the role and importance of universities and other higher education institutions, and research and science, across the world. Corresponding to CGHE's projects, monographs in the series will consist of social science research on global, international, national and local aspects of higher education, drawing on methodologies in education, learning theory, sociology, economics, political science and policy studies. Monographs will be prepared so as to maximise worldwide readership and selected on the basis of their relevance to one or more of higher education policy, management, practice and theory. Topics will range from teaching and learning and technologies, to research and research impact in industry, national system design, the public good role of universities, social stratification and equity, institutional governance and management, and the cross-border mobility of people, institutions, programmes, ideas and knowledge. The Bloomsbury Higher Education Research series is at the cutting edge of world research on higher education.

Advisory Board:

Paul Blackmore, King's College London, UK; Brendan Cantwell, Michigan State University, USA; Gwilym Croucher, University of Melbourne, Australia; Carolina Guzman-Valenzuela, University of Chile, Chile; Glen Jones, University of Toronto, Canada; Barbara Kehm, University of Glasgow, UK; Jenny Lee, University of Arizona, USA; Ye Liu, King's College London, UK; Christine Musselin, Sciences Po, France; Alis Oancea, University of Oxford, UK; Imanol Ordorika, Universidad Nacional Autónoma de México, Mexico; Laura Perna, University of Pennsylvania, USA; Gary Rhoades, University of Arizona, USA; Susan Robertson, University of Cambridge, UK; Yang Rui, University of Hong Kong, Hong Kong; Pedro Teixeira, University of Porto, Portugal; Jussi Valimaa, University of Jyvaskyla, Finland; N.V. Varghese, National University of Educational Planning and Administration, India; Marijk van der Wende, University of Utrecht, The Netherlands; Po Yang, Peking University, China; Akiyoshi Yonezawa, Tohoku University, Japan

Also available in the series:

The Governance of British Higher Education: The Impact of Governmental, Financial and Market Pressures, Michael Shattock and Aniko Horvath

Changing Higher Education for a Changing World, edited by Claire Callender, William Locke and Simon Marginson

Changing Higher Education in India, edited by Saumen Chattopadhyay, Simon Marginson and N.V. Varghese

Changing Higher Education in East Asia, Simon Marginson and Xin Xu

Higher Education, State and Society, Lili Yang

Forthcoming in the series:

Challenging Approaches to Academic Career-Making, Celia Whitchurch, William Locke and Giulio Marini

Universities and Regions: The Impact of Locality and Region on University Governance and Strategies, Michael Shattock and Aniko Horvath

The Governance of European Higher Education

Convergence or Divergence?

Michael Shattock, Aniko Horvath and Jurgen Enders

BLOOMSBURY ACADEMIC
LONDON • NEW YORK • OXFORD • NEW DELHI • SYDNEY

BLOOMSBURY ACADEMIC
Bloomsbury Publishing Plc
50 Bedford Square, London, WC1B 3DP, UK
1385 Broadway, New York, NY 10018, USA
29 Earlsfort Terrace, Dublin 2, Ireland

BLOOMSBURY, BLOOMSBURY ACADEMIC and the Diana logo
are trademarks of Bloomsbury Publishing Plc

First published in Great Britain 2023
Paperback edition published 2024

Copyright © Michael Shattock, Aniko Horvath and Jurgen Enders, 2023

Michael Shattock, Aniko Horvath and Jurgen Enders have asserted their right under the Copyright, Designs and Patents Act, 1988, to be identified as Author of this work.

For legal purposes the Acknowledgements on p. xiii constitute
an extension of this copyright page.

Series design by Adriana Brioso
Cover image © Setthasith Wansuksri/EyeEm/Getty Images

All rights reserved. No part of this publication may be reproduced or transmitted in any form or by any means, electronic or mechanical, including photocopying, recording, or any information storage or retrieval system, without prior permission in writing from the publishers.

Bloomsbury Publishing Plc does not have any control over, or responsibility for, any third-party websites referred to or in this book. All internet addresses given in this book were correct at the time of going to press. The author and publisher regret any inconvenience caused if addresses have changed or sites have ceased to exist, but can accept no responsibility for any such changes.

A catalogue record for this book is available from the British Library.

Library of Congress Cataloging-in-Publication Data

Names: Shattock, Michael, author. | Horvath, Aniko, author. | Enders, Jürgen, author.
Title: The governance of European higher education : convergence or divergence? / Michael Shattock, Aniko Horvath and Jurgen Enders.
Description: New York, NY : Bloomsbury Academic, 2023. |
Series: Bloomsbury higher education research |
Includes bibliographical references and index.
Identifiers: LCCN 2022046937 (print) | LCCN 2022046938 (ebook) |
ISBN 9781350293564 (hardback) | ISBN 9781350293601 (paperback) |
ISBN 9781350293571 (adobe pdf) | ISBN 9781350293588 (epub)
Subjects: LCSH: Universities and colleges–Europe–Administration. |
Education, Higher–Europe–Administration. | Higher education and state–Europe.
Classification: LCC LB2341.8.E85 S53 2023 (print) |
LCC LB2341.8.E85 (ebook) | DDC 378.4–dc23/eng/20221005
LC record available at https://lccn.loc.gov/2022046937
LC ebook record available at https://lccn.loc.gov/2022046938

ISBN: HB: 978-1-3502-9356-4
PB: 978-1-3502-9360-1
ePDF: 978-1-3502-9357-1
eBook: 978-1-3502-9358-8

Series: Bloomsbury Higher Education Research

Typeset by Integra Software Services Pvt. Ltd.

To find out more about our authors and books visit www.bloomsbury.com
and sign up for our newsletters.

Contents

Series Editor's Foreword	viii
Acknowledgements	xiii
List of Acronyms	xiv
Introduction	1
1 The State and the Institutions	9
2 Institutional Diversification, Regional Disparities and System Management	55
3 The 'modernization' of Institutional Governance	79
4 The Changing Participation of Students and Staff in the Governance of European Universities	113
5 The Changing Idea and Role of Universities in Europe	155
6 Convergence and Divergence in the Developing Governance of European Higher Education	177
References	185
Works Cited	188
Index	193

Series Editor's Foreword

The Governance of European Higher Education: Convergence or Divergence? is the sixth book to be published in the Bloomsbury Higher Education Research book series. This series brings to the public, government and universities across the world the new ideas and research evidence being generated by researchers from the ESRC/OFSRE Centre for Global Higher Education[*]. The Centre for Global Higher Education (CGHE), a partnership of researchers from eleven UK and international universities, is the world's largest concentration of expertise in relation to higher education and its social contributions. The core focus of CGHE's work, and of the Bloomsbury Higher Education Research Series, is higher education, especially the future of higher education in the changing global landscape.

Each year this mega-topic of 'higher education' seems to take on greater importance for governments, business, civil organizations, students, families and the public at large. In higher education much is at stake. The role and impact of the sector are growing everywhere. More than 235 million students enrol at tertiary level across the world, four-fifths of them in degree programmes. Over 40 per cent of school leavers now enter some kind of tertiary education each year, though resources and quality vary significantly. In North America and Europe that ratio rises to four young people in every five. Universities and colleges are seen as the primary medium for personal opportunity, social mobility and the development of whole communities. About 2.5 million new science papers are published worldwide each year, and the role of research in industry and government continues to expand everywhere.

In short, there is much at stake in higher education. It has become central to social, economic, cultural and political life. One reason is that even while serving local society and national policy, the higher education and research sectors are especially globalized in character. Each year six million students change countries in order to enrol in their chosen study programme, and a quarter of all published research papers involve joint authorship across national borders. In some countries fee-based international education is a major source of export revenues, while some other countries are losing talent in net terms each year. Routine cross-border movements of students, academics and researchers, knowledge, information and money help to shape not only nations but the international order itself.

At the same time, the global higher education landscape is changing with compelling speed, reflecting larger economic, political and cultural shifts in the geo-strategic setting. Though research universities in the United States (especially) and the UK remain strong in comparative terms, the worldwide map of power in higher education is becoming more plural. A larger range of higher education practices, including models of teaching/learning, delivery, institutional organization and system, will shape higher education in future. Anglo-American (and Western) norms and models will be less dominant and will themselves evolve. Rising universities and science in East Asia and Singapore are already reshaping the flow of knowledge and higher education. Latin America, Southeast Asia, India, Central Asia and the Arab nations have a growing global importance. The trajectories of education and research in sub-Saharan Africa are crucial to state-building and community development.

All of this has led to a more intensive focus on how higher education systems and institutions function and their value, performance, effectiveness, openness and sustainability. This in turn has made research on higher education more significant – both because it provides us with insights into one important facet of the human condition and because it informs evidenced-based government policies and professional practices.

CGHE opened in late 2015 and is currently funded until October 2023. The centre investigates higher education using a range of social science disciplines including economics, sociology, political science and policy studies, psychology and anthropology, and uses a portfolio of quantitative, qualitative and synthetic-historical research techniques. It currently maintains ten research projects, variously of between eighteen months and eight years' duration, as well as smaller projects, and involves about forty active affiliated individual researchers. Over its eight-year span it is financed by about £10 million in funding from the UK Economic and Social Research Council, partner universities and other sources. Its UK researchers are drawn from the Universities of Oxford, Lancaster, Surrey, Bath and University College London. The headquarters of the centre are located at Oxford, and there are large concentrations of researchers at both Oxford and UCL. The current affiliated international researchers are from Hiroshima University in Japan, Shanghai Jiao Tong University in China, Lingnan University in Hong Kong, Cape Town University in South Africa, Virginia Tech in the United States and Technological University Dublin. CGHE also collaborates with researchers from many other universities across the world, in seminars, conferences and exchange of papers. It runs an active programme of global webinars.

The centre has a full agenda. The unprecedented growth of mass higher education, the striving for excellence and innovation in the research university sector and the changing global landscape pose many researchable questions for governments, societies and higher education institutions themselves. Some of these questions already figure in CGHE research projects. For example: What are the formative effects on societies and economies of the now much wider distribution of advanced levels of learning? How does it change individual graduates as people – and what does it mean when half or more of the workforce is higher educated and much more mobile; and when confident human agency has become widely distributed across civil and political society in nations with little state tradition, or where the main experience has been colonial or authoritarian rule? What does it mean when many more people are becoming steeped in the sciences, many others understand the world through the lenses of the social sciences or humanities, and a third group are engaged in neither? What happens to those parts of the population left outside the formative effects of higher education? What is the larger public role and contribution of higher education, as distinct from the private benefits for and private effects on individual graduates? What does it mean when large and growing higher education institutions have become the major employers in many locations and help to sustain community and cultural life, almost like branches of local government while also being linked to global cities across the world? And what is the contribution of higher education, beyond helping to form the attributes of individual graduates, to the development of the emerging global society?

Likewise, the many practical problems associated with building higher education and science take on greater importance. How can scarce public budgets provide for the public role of higher education institutions, for a socially equitable system of individual access and for research excellence, all at the same time? What is the role for and limits of family financing and tuition loans systems? What is the potential contribution of private institutions, including for-profit colleges? In national systems, what is the best balance between research-intensive and primarily teaching institutions, and between academic and vocational education? What are the potentials for technological delivery in extending access? What is happening in graduate labour markets, where returns to degrees are becoming more dispersed between families with differing levels of income, different kinds universities and different fields of study? Do larger education systems provide better for social mobility and income equality? How does the internationalization of universities contribute to national policy and local societies? Does mobile international education expand opportunity or further stratify societies? What are the implications of new populist tensions between national and global goals, as manifest for example in the tensions over Brexit in the UK and the politics of the Trump era in the United States, for higher education and research? And always, what can national systems of higher education and science learn from each other, and how can they build stronger common ground?

In tackling these research challenges and bringing the research to all, we are very grateful to have the opportunity to work with such a high-quality publisher as Bloomsbury. In the book series monographs are selected on the basis of their relevance to one or more of higher education policy, management, practice and theory. Topics range from teaching and learning and technologies, to research and its organization, the design parameters of national higher education systems, the public good role of higher education, social stratification and equity, institutional governance and management, and the cross-border mobility of people, programmes and ideas. Much of CGHE's work is global and comparative in scale, drawing lessons from higher education in many different countries, and the centre's cross-country and multi-project structure allows it to tap into the more plural higher education and research landscape that has emerged. The book series draws on authors from across the world and is prepared for relevance across the world.

CGHE places special emphasis on the relevance of its research, on communicating its findings and on maximizing the usefulness and impacts of those findings in higher education policy and practice. CGHE has a relatively high public profile for an academic research centre and reaches out to engage higher education stakeholders, national and international organizations, policymakers, regulators and the broader public, in the UK and across the world. These objectives are also central to the book series. Recognizing that the translation from research outputs to high-quality scholarly monographs is not always straightforward – while achieving impact in both academic and policy/practice circles is crucial – monographs in the book series are scrutinized critically before publication, for readability as well as quality. Texts are carefully written and edited to ensure that they have achieved the right combination of, on the one hand, intellectual depth and originality, and on the other hand, full accessibility for public, higher education and policy circles across the world.

Simon Marginson
Professor of Higher Education, University of Oxford
Director, ESRC/OFSRE Centre for Global Higher Education

Note

* The initials ESRC/OFSRE stand for the Economic and Social Research Council/Office for Students and Research England. Part of the original ESRC funding that supported the Centre for Global Higher Education's research work was sourced from the Higher Education Funding Council for England, the ancestor body to the OFS and RE. Research England continues to provide financial support for the research.

Acknowledgements

We wish to begin by thanking the institutions in the five countries and their members who gave their time to us and also to the policymakers who gave us the benefit of their experience and knowledge of events. In addition we wish to acknowledge particularly Professor Christine Musselin and Professor Roberto Moscati, eminent authorities in the field, for interviews in relation to higher education developments in France and Italy which gave context to our work in the five countries we selected for special study. The research was carried out under the auspices of the Centre for Global Higher Education at Oxford (Director, Professor Simon Marginson). It is important to place on record that the Centre's funding provided a unique opportunity in the present financial climate for this kind of detailed empirical research in higher education in five continental European countries as well as in the UK. We are very grateful to Simon for his constant support and encouragement for the project. We are also most grateful to Alison Baker at Bloomsbury for her support for publication and her patience in respect to the timing of its completion. Finally we would like to express our thanks to our Hungarian, German and British transcribers, as well as to our Hungarian and German translators, for transcribing and translating the interviews, and to Caroline Steenman-Clark, who prepared the majority of the material for manuscript submission. We acknowledge with gratitude the funding support of the Economic and Social Research Council and Research England (Grant reference ES/MO10082/1).

Acronyms

ANR	National Research Agency (France)
BEIS	Department for Business, Energy and Industrial Strategy (UK)
BIS	Department for Business, Innovation and Skills (UK)
CAT	College of Advanced Technology
CNAA	Council for National Academic Awards
CRNS	Centre National de la Recherche Scientifique (France)
CUC	Committee of University Chairs
CVCP	Committee of Vice-Chancellors and Principals
DES	Department of Education and Science (UK)
DFG	Deutsche Forschungsgemeinschaft (Germany)
DIUS	Department of Innovation, Universities and Skills (UK)
DTI	Department of Trade and Industry (UK)
ELTE	Eotvos Lorand University
ENQA	European Association for Quality Assurance
ESU	European Student Union
EU	European Union
EUA	European Universities Association
HAC	Hungarian Accreditation Committee
HEFCE	Higher Education Funding Council for England
HEFCW	Higher Education Funding Council for Wales

IDEX	Initiative d'Excellence
IUT	Institut Universitaire de Technologie
LOPRI	Loi pour la recherche et l'innovation
NCSU	National Committee of Student Unions (Hungary)
NFST	National Foundation for Science and Technology (Portugal)
NOKUT	Norwegian Agency for Quality Assurance in Education
NRDIO	National Research, Development and Innovation Office
NSS	National Student Survey
NUS	National Union of Students (UK)
OECD	Organisation for Economic Cooperation and Development
OfS	Office for Students (UK)
PRES	Pole de Recherche et d'enseignement superior
QAA	Quality Assurance Agency
RAE	Research Assessment Exercise
RCN	Norwegian Research Council
REF	Research Excellence Framework
SFC	Scottish Funding Council
SWO	Student Welfare Organization (Norway)
UGC	University Grants Committee
UTAD	University of Tras os Montes e Alto Doura
UK	United Kingdom
UUK	Universities UK

Introduction

This book forms a complementary volume to *The Governance of British Higher Education: The Impact of Governmental, Financial and Market Pressures* (Shattock and Horvath, Bloomsbury Academic, 2019), for which its research programme has also been funded by the Economic and Social Research Council (ESRC), and Research England through the Centre for Global Higher Education at Oxford. We take it for granted that the study of European higher education must include the UK. Politically the UK may have left the European Union but its academic, intellectual and cultural traditions have historically been closely related to university systems on the European continent. The UK was a key signatory to the Bologna Declaration in 1999 – it had been one of only four European states which had combined to issue its predecessor, the Sorbonne Declaration, in 1998 which called for the harmonization of the architecture of European higher education – and of the creation of the European Higher Education Area in 2010; the restructuring of the common European degree framework through the Bologna Process adopted the English three-year first degree as the first cycle of the 3+2+3 sequence of degrees. In 2017–18, 12 per cent of the staff of UK universities were drawn from continental Europe, 6 per cent of students were from continental Europe and, thanks to EU Framework and Horizon grants, the UK has been a leading collaborator in research with universities on the continent; the UK aims to continue to be a member of the EU Horizon programme.

The fact that the UK has left the European Union, and is likely not to seek any change in that position for many years if ever, does not, and is not likely to, affect the very strong cultural affinities which bind the Europe of the EU and the UK together. From a policy point of view it is also useful to view UK higher education through a European lens rather than as a disaffiliated country because the comparative perspective throws up the fact that policy differences and governance practices between EU countries, as also between their economic and political cultures, are in many ways no less extreme than those which differentiate the four Anglophone nations within the UK from nations within the EU (or like Norway, which is strongly affiliated through policy and practice with the EU).

For their UK project, Shattock and Horvath conducted ninety-five interviews with central policymakers and in depth with thirteen universities; these universities were chosen to represent the very diverse UK institutional landscape. Six of the institutional interview programmes were carried out in Scotland, Wales and Northern Ireland and seven in England. One of the findings of the UK research was the extent to which, post-devolution, Scottish and Welsh higher education systems have diverged from that in England. Accordingly, this book, while recognizing the inherited commonalities of having once being part of a unified UK system, treats English, Scottish and Welsh higher education as separate systems for comparison with national systems in continental Europe. (We have not included Northern Ireland, the fourth devolved system in the UK, because of the small size of the system, with only two universities, and because its structure is essentially unchanged since before devolution.)

For the European project, Horvath and Enders conducted eighty-eight interviews with central policymakers in Germany, Hungary, Norway and Portugal and interviewed in depth in two case study universities in each country, chosen, as in the UK, to represent the diversity of the university systems. The interviews were based on the template of questions developed for the UK case study universities and were complemented by some additional questions to account for possible particulars in each country. The relative sizes of the seven countries by population are as follows: Germany 83 million, England 55 million, Hungary 9.7 million, Norway 5.3 million, Portugal 10.2 million, Scotland 5.5 million and Wales 3 million.

In selecting countries from continental Europe, we tried to identify representative higher education systems: Germany's is the largest and the inheritor of the most enduring European governance model, the Humboldtian tradition; in addition we selected Norway as a representative 'northern' nation and Hungary as representative of central and east European universities emerging after 1989 from communist dominated systems (both, as it happens, historically influenced by Humboldtian tradition). Finally we chose Portugal as a representative 'southern' European system. As our findings demonstrate their governance profiles are very different. To supplement them and to broaden our comparators we drew on two scholars, Professor Christine Musselin for France and Professor Roberto Moscati for Italy, to give us up-to-date accounts of developments in their own systems. The French system is important in illustrating how the Napoleonic model, which heavily influenced Italy, Spain and Portugal, is losing its historic relevance in the modernizing reforms now being undertaken there. Italy, a large European system in its own right offers a helpful comparison to the context in Portugal as another southern European university system.

We have also been fortunate to be able to draw on a wealth of scholarly material produced over the last decade or so: *Progress in Higher Education Reform in Europe Part I Governance Reform* de Boer, H, Jongblood, B, Enders, J, and File, J (CHEPS 2009); *University Governance Western European Perspectives* Paradeise, C, Reale, E, Bleike, I, Ferlie, E (Springer 2009); *International Trends in University Governance* Shattock, M.L (Ed) (Routledge 2014); *Managing Universities, Policy and Organizational Change from a Western European Perspective* Bleike, I, Enders, J, and Lapori, B, (Macmillan 2017); *Governance Reforms in European University Systems: The Case of Austria, Denmark, Finland, France, the Netherlands and Portugal* Kruger, K, Parallada, M, Samoilivich, D, and Sursock, A (Eds) (Springer 2018). One could mention many articles and book chapters on comparative themes or on individual country systems but reference must be made in respect to contributions on two of the major European systems: Germany – Teichler, U, 'Germany: Continuous Intergovernmental Negotiations' in Carnoy, M, Froumin, I, Leshukov, O, and Marginson, S (Eds) *Higher Education in Federal Countries: A Comparative Study* Springer – and France – 'The Impact of Recent Reforms in the Institutional Governance of French Universities' Chartelain-Ponroy, S, Mignot-Gerard, S, Musselin, C, and Sporiam, S, in Shattock *op cit* 2014 together with an extended recorded conversation with Professor Musselin bringing this analysis up to date.

While our selection of countries and universities for special study was not, and for practical purposes could not be, comprehensive, we believe that the spread of our selection, together with the accounts of developments in France and Italy, and the depths of the interviews with policymakers and within institutions, makes it legitimate to generalize about Euopean higher education as a whole. In addition, while the research findings rest heavily on the empirical studies we have undertaken, we have been able to draw on a wider literature on European higher education and on ideas about European higher education itself which have enlarged our perspective on the European scene. As a result we believe that the conclusions we draw in Chapter 6 can be seen as representative pointers of the development and trends to be found in the broad span of European higher education.

An important theme in the book is the question of whether European governance structures, at national and institutional levels, are converging or diverging and whether there is any kind of consistent change in the idea of a European university. Chapter 1 explores the roots of the dominant European university system models, the Humboldtian, the Napoleonic and the Anglophone. It is clear from our interviews that while the Humboldtian remains influential, the Napoleonic and the Anglophone are subject to significant change as wide-ranging reforms are introduced. These changes are not bottom up but top down and are government-led, reflecting national government priorities much more than those which might, in other circumstances, have sprung from the systems themselves or been introduced by autonomous institutions.

Our findings suggest that rather than moving towards a greater convergence of systems or towards some kind of unified pattern of governance styles, systems have a tendency to diverge from common models as they evolve; there has been no transforming Bologna Process for higher education governance. As modernizing reforms take place they seem to be moving systems closer to national governments' political priorities and to responding to distinct national geophysical characteristics and away from a unique European model. This is not to say that convergence is not taking place but it is often unconscious as countries confront similar issues in similar ways. The picture is more rather than less divergent than it was a decade ago.

The chapters are briefly summarized below:

Chapter 1 The state and the institutions

This chapter addresses the relationship between the state and higher education in Europe and is primarily directed towards how this is mediated through system governance. The chapter is divided into two parts. The first concerns the balance between continuities and change and describes how the three major organizational models, the Humboldtian, the Napoleonic and the Anglophone, while continuing to remain embedded in national systems and to frame system development, are losing their distinctiveness under the pressures of massification, the needs of the knowledge economy, regional disparities and international change. The second part compares how governments have acted to seek to modernize their systems, adapt them to meet regional demands, respond to the reputational impact of international institutional rankings and adjust to the reforms consequent on the Bologna Process. These themes are explored by comparing system change/system rationalization across Europe. A central conclusion is that across widely different systems the state is becoming more directive and interventionist in respect to institutional autonomy.

Chapter 2 Institutional diversification, regional disparities and system management

Massification in student numbers across European countries has led to a diversification in institutional models. This diversification has been accentuated in some countries by the demands to extend higher education to regions rather than being concentrated in historic centres. Initially this led to the establishment of two-tier systems, polytechnics, regional colleges and Fachhochschulen, where university status was protected by what became known as binary lines. Over time this demarcation became eroded and challenged as representing inequitable divisions between institutions teaching, following Bologna, to common degree levels. Compromises were reached with institutional mergers and upgradings and the introduction of 'university of applied science' titles, the criteria for the latter tending to vary slightly between nations. Diversities within systems were increased by requirements as to whether these new institutions should also be research active. The chapter shows how system rationalization and realignment of institutions have brought with them greater differentiation away from a common model of European structures.

Chapter 3 The 'modernization' of institutional governance

This chapter describes the evolution of governance at the institutional level and particularly the move across all European countries to strengthen university management decision-making structures. There has been great variation but the processes have tended to concentrate in continental Europe on the introduction of external (lay) members into institutional governance and on the authority of institutions' central management, the heads of universities and their executive teams. In the UK, where lay involvement has been a traditional component of university governance, the trend has been to reinforce the roles of governing bodies at the expense of academic senates. In continental Europe, except in Hungary, the results have been more mixed: lay majorities on governing bodies are less common, and the powers of rectors continue to be circumscribed by the devolved powers of deans and faculties. While, therefore, most continental universities continue to exercise a significant degree of academic control over decision-making, in the UK, and to a considerable extent in Hungary, the role of the academic community has become more limited.

Chapter 4 The changing participation of students and staff in the governance of European universities

There have been considerable changes in the main components of institutional governance across European higher education. This chapter describes the changing balance of the contribution of students and academic staff. Thus while in the UK and in Hungary the involvement of the academic community in decision-making has been weakened, although in different ways, in the rest of continental Europe the autonomy of faculties and the power to elect their own deans leave governing bodies, rectors and executive teams less freedom in decision-making. On the other hand, the student body in continental universities has a more prominent role in governance with greater voting powers and a more political role in the affairs of the university. The tendency in all countries is for a more top-down form of governance but it remains the case that academic staff continue to control the governance of teaching although in Hungary and Portugal the process of external accreditation severely challenges the autonomy of institutions.

Chapter 5 The changing idea and role of universities in Europe

The previous chapters describe empirically the forces that have brought change to the architectures of European higher education; this chapter sums up the effects on institutions. It shows how we are witnessing possibly the end of the idea that the university deserves financial support because of what it is but rather than for what it does and what it achieves. This has involved a process of 'demystification' of the idea of the university and the growth of the concept of the university as a 'corporate actor' transformed from a 'loosely' to a 'tightly coupled' system. This has led to hybrid forms of the university as a managed professional organization, a model that comes in different shapes depending on the national and organizational context. With massification, higher education has become a much broader church with mission stretch from 'world class' to second- or third-tier regional universities. A more utilitarian idea of the university has prompted states to become more active in seeking to rationalize and 'modernize' their higher education systems.

Chapter 6 Convergence and divergence in the developing governance of European higher education

This chapter argues that convergence and divergence may be said to be occurring simultaneously and that superficial descriptions of the establishment of new approaches to system management may overlay profound differences in political and social character. It finds that there is general convergence in the evidence of more interventionist approaches to governance by the state: the decision in England to dispense with a neutral intermediary body and permit a much closer engagement with a minister puts it much closer to a continental model. A strengthening of management structures in universities and the introduction or reinforcement of lay members in institutional governance represents common themes. Against this divergence in restructuring to cope with massification and 'hinterland' issues, in research policies and, in particular, in respect to funding and performativity measures all reflect differing national priorities. The drive for a European governance model seems to have run its course: the future is likely to bring increasing divergence.

The book is jointly authored, with Michael Shattock taking primary responsibility for Chapters 1, 2, 3 and 6, Aniko Horvath for Chapter 4 and Jurgen Enders for Chapter 5.

1

The State and the Institutions

Continuities and change in the governance of European higher education

The Napoleonic, Humboldtian and Anglophone patterns

The period since 2000 has seen major changes in the governance of European higher education. De Boer and Enders (2017) offer a general proposition as to the process which was set in train:

> The traditional steering model with strong state control and weak organisational control was intended to be replaced with a model in which the state was steering from a distance and organisations were 'empowered' in several ways to determine their own destiny.

It has not altogether worked out in this way as the evidence quoted in the following chapters will show; state intervention has been common and disruptive. De Boer and Enders make the important point that autonomy has been strongly circumscribed by universities' financial dependence on the state and the state bureaucracy which accompanies it. But, lying behind the changes and reforms, continuities in governance can still influence organizational cultures, or simply the ways things are done, both at state and institutional levels. Relationships between states and institutions, institutional hierarchies and academic practices become embedded and carry weight long after reforms which demand that they change are implemented; academic institutions like universities are difficult to change, the fundamentals of teaching and research provide an accepted framework for the conduct of the core business: who takes a decision on particular academic issues – a head of department, a dean or a rector – and with what degree of corporate responsibility at faculty, at senate or at some higher body – are prescribed by custom and habit as much as by regulation or legislation. A lecture today in the Sorbonne or in the Humboldt University or in Oxford looks much like it did in 1900 or even 1800; quality measures, accreditation machinery and performance assessment may be invoked but the essential functions of universities persist very much as they always did.

Historically, higher education governance structures in Europe developed in three main patterns: the Napoleonic, the Humboldtian and the Anglophone. In 1793 Napoleon suppressed the existing French universities, leaving faculties as self-standing organizations, but in 1806 he created a single university controlled from Paris composed of both lycées and the previous faculties. Ninety years later legislation recreated the universities but the discipline-based faculties remained as described in Chatelain-Portnoy *et al.* (2014) as 'the main pillars of the French system and the natural interlocutors of the Ministry'. The Napoleonic model was characterized by the dominance of government (under Napoleon the chief officer of the single university reported direct to the head of state) and a low level of institutional autonomy (a ministry was only established in 1828). Academically the university had a focus on professional and vocational studies, training for service in the state bureaucracy, and had a strong concentration on teaching at the expense of research. Chatelain-Portnoy *et al.* (2014) show that the creation of the Centre National de la Recherche Scientifique (CRNS) in 1936, a body entirely devoted to research, was dictated by the absence of research in French universities. The French model was imposed on those other countries which had come under Napoleonic rule: Italy, Portugal and Spain. As testimony to its continuing influence in Portugal a senior Portuguese university figure told us:

> We don't have a tradition of regulation, we have a tradition of control because in terms of public administration there was this Napoleonic tradition, very strong, which of course was reinforced by having a very strong state throughout the twentieth century... this tradition of the State... is still embedded in the system in some ways. (1)

By contrast the task of the state in the Humboldtian model was to protect the universities' academic freedom and not to impose arbitrary controls over them. Equally important, the essence of the Humboldtian model was the inter-relationship of teaching and research. Humboldt persuaded the king of Prussia to reject the application of the Napoleonic reforms to follow the liberal ideas of the philosopher Schleiermacher, who argued that a university's function was not to pass on recognized and directly usable knowledge as in schools but to demonstrate how knowledge is discovered: ' to stimulate the idea of science in the minds of the students, to encourage them to take account of the fundamental laws of science in all their thinking' (quoted in Ruegg, W 2004 p 5). In governance the Humboldtian ideal was to give universities considerable operational autonomy but to retain them as part of the state, with professors paid as public servants and a member of the public service acting as *Kanzler,* answerable to government, effectively a legal officer acting to ensure the university followed state regulations. This structure remains partly intact: while the government specifies university constitutions and their governance components, University Acts emphasize institutional autonomy but permit variations between Länder as to the precise inter-relationships of their governance machinery. On the other hand the federal government has taken on an additional responsibility:

> The German education system was historically developed and is bound by the responsibility for performance which is legitimised under constitutional law... here in Germany the federal government has been involved in the responsibility for performance at schools and universities from the beginning. (senior state officer) (2)

Founded in 1810, the Humboldt University provided the model for a reform of universities in Germany and in Austria and in Northern, and in East and Central Europe. In Hungary, for example, interviewees made frequent reference to their system's Humboldtian past interrupted by the years of Soviet influence. Thus the rector of a major Hungarian university chose to define his university's Humboldtian academic mission in the words: 'there is no excuse to be excellent in education [teaching] but doing nothing in research, so this is the Humboldtian model which we aim to follow' (3). In Norway a senior university figure described to us a relationship between universities and the state which almost replicated the original Humboldtian model:

> We are part of the public state structure and in that sense we are subordinate to the Ministry of Research and Education and that means we cannot borrow money as an independent actor. We have special autonomy, given that we are a university, but we are definitely part of the state structure and we have the state auditor come and check how we spend public money. (4)

Another Norwegian interviewee, in response to a question about how closely the universities and the government seemed to work together, commented:

> They do… but I think the UK is often viewed as a sort of scary example from our side because… in the Norwegian model there is a lot of dialogue and there is quite a close connection between the leadership [of the universities] and the Ministry in the sense that they have a style of meetings for steering [the system], and autonomy is always in the discussion….There is a strong emphasis on dialogue. (5)

The Ministry and the universities can be described as acting as partners in a common enterprise.

Such a relationship would never have been attainable in the UK, and certainly not in England now, or for most of the time in the last century where universities have always defended their independence robustly against suspected encroachments by the state. Those English and Welsh universities that had their origins in the nineteenth century were founded by private citizens for largely local and regional purposes, not by the state, and cherished their academic freedoms albeit, from the perspective of continental European universities of the period, they were circumscribed, as none of the continental universities were, by external (lay) members sitting in a majority on their governing bodies. In Scotland the 'ancient' universities (Edinburgh, Glasgow, Aberdeen and St Andrews) were created by various bodies, religious and civic, but in no case by the state itself. In the Anglophone model, universities were free to pursue teaching and research without external controls, appointed their own staff including the head of the university on their own conditions of service, selected their own students, owned their own estates and maintained their buildings at their own expense. They also raised their own funding, although increasingly they came to depend in part on supplementary grants from the state.

In 1919, at the end of the First World War, UK universities appealed for more regular funding which the government agreed should be provided through the mechanism of a University Grants Committee (UGC), which was specifically designed to protect universities' academic and financial autonomy from possible influence by government. The committee was made up of a majority of academics and the funding, which amounted to only about 30 per cent of individual universities' annual income, was made available on a deficiency grant basis, that is, to make up their private funding to a level which enabled them to meet their academic needs. Only in 1946, in the light of the effects of the Second World War and the influx of an expanded student population, did the universities become fully funded by the government through a reformed UGC which, while appointed by the government, continued to be a body dominated by an academic membership (Shattock 1994). The UGC's independence from government led it to be described as acting like 'a collective Minister' (Carswell 1985). Even as late as the 1980s formal Letters of Guidance from the Secretary of State to the UGC were often drafted in the chairman's office.

Both the government and the university system saw the UGC as a 'buffer' between the government and the universities. No continental European system had this kind of intermediary body: relationships were always direct with a ministry and, in most cases, while academic autonomy was vested in the institutions, sites and buildings continued to be owned by the state, staff were appointed on public service terms and rectors were elected by the staff rather than appointed in open competition. Thus the UK system stands out in comparison with the rest of Europe in the kind of legal and substantive autonomy its universities enjoyed and in its arms-length relationship with government, a condition confirmed in the European Universities Association (EUA) *Autonomy Scorecards* of 2011 (Estermann *et al.*) and 2017 (EUA).

The historic patterns modified by national 'modernization' strategies

Although the historic freedom from government control that UK universities enjoyed became increasingly restricted with the abolition of the UGC in 1989 and its replacement in 1992 by Higher Education Funding Councils for England, Scotland and Wales (HEFCE, SFC and HEFCW), the Anglophone concept of institutional autonomy and associated internal constitutional and management structures was embedded in the universities and in the system. However, the trend towards greater government control has increased. While intermediary bodies have been retained in Scotland and Wales HEFCE has been replaced in England by a regulator, the Office for Students (OfS), with the government choosing to manage the English university system by the application of a highly regulated adherence to market principles punctuated by ministerial interventions (Shattock and Horvath 2019). The change represents a sharp reversal of the original principles of the Anglophone model and, arguably, the most extreme departure in any European country from its structure two decades ago.

Both France and Italy have also seen significant modifications to their original models, in each case led, following the Napoleonic tradition, by the state. In France a series of game-changing pieces of legislation have reshaped the university system and reduced its historic fragmentation between grandes écoles, universities and detached faculty campuses: *Pôle de recherche et d'enseignement supérieur* (PRES) in 2007 promoted joining together universities and grandes écoles located in the same region, *Libertés et Responsabilités des Universités*, published in the same year, gave universities greater operational autonomy, including devolving the salary budget to universities, and further legislation in 2013 set new legal statutes to replace the existing PRES and increased coordination at the regional level, reshaping the university system. Even more significant was the new emphasis given to research in universities, in direct contrast to the original Napoleonic model, with the *Loi pour la recherche et l'innovation* (LOPRI) in 2006 and the *Initiative d'Excellence* (IDEX) in 2010, which offered new competitive funding based on research quality but only to universities which had engaged positively in PRES. An important element of the reforms was to strengthen the position of the university president to carry through these initiatives. One other characteristic of a changed French approach was the new willingness of the government to consult the university system before engaging in top-down reform. Thus M. Hollande, the then French president, embarked on a national consultation, the *Alises Nationales de l'Enseignement Supérieur et de la Recherche*, prior to the 2013 legislation and extensive dialogues took place with the Rectors' Conference before subsequent legislation in 2017 (Chartelain-Ponroy et al. 2014, Musselin private communication). Italy has moved in a similar direction with legislation in 1989 and 2014 which has redefined corporate governance and increased accountability, strengthened executive leadership, introduced a block grant funding system and established a research evaluation exercise which has encouraged institutional ranking and competition (Moscati 2014 and private communication). As a result of state-directed reform both French and Italian higher education systems have moved substantially away from their Napoleonic roots.

The modification of the historic patterns of governance that we see in England, and in France and Italy, is mirrored in other countries usually but not exclusively consequential on political and other factors external to the universities. In Portugal the reliance on state control, which it inherited from its Napoleonic past, was enhanced under the Salazar dictatorship but transformed after the 1974–6 Revolution, which threw out the *ancien* regime. Education came to be seen as 'an avenue of social mobility rather than a threat to the income of the traditional rural family by luring individuals away to the city' (Neave and Amaral 2012, p. 25). Higher education became 'wedded to an agenda firmly rooted in the application and extension of Participative Democracy to academia' (Neave and Amaral 2012, p. 26). The 1988 University Autonomy Act terminated the existing system of autocratic management and what Cardoso described at the time as the 'long lasting and humiliating dependence on political power' (Cardoso 1989, p. 132 as cited in Gonçalves 2012). In 2007, heavily influenced by the European Union's state supervisory model, the government passed a Higher Education Guideline Act which promised a transfer of universities to 'foundation status' and the appointment of boards of trustees to be interposed between the ministry and academic leadership. Research became a key function of the university system, as in France: 'surely', said one dean interviewed, 'nowadays everyone knows that they are expected to do research' (6). Nevertheless old habits die hard: the state continues to exercise strong regulatory controls and foundation status has proved to be less effective in promoting institutional self-government than promised: according to one interviewee:

> We were supposed not to be under such strict control but it [has not yet happened]. Each government says, oh yes this is the law but for this year we will like this, constrain this, constrain this, constrain this so by the end of the day there is no difference between being a public foundation as we are or being a regular university. (7)

In Germany, after 1946, the country was decentralized through devolution to the Länder, which passed the direct control of universities away from central government. This could have led to a diversification of the university system away from the Humboldtian model if individual Länder had been inclined to do so but they were constrained by two factors: first, the provision in the federal constitution which imposed the principle of the maintenance of 'homogeneous living conditions' between the Länder and, second, as described by Teichler (2018), the Länder's own self-restraint in being unwilling to contemplate any major structural changes without close consultation with one another. When reunification took place in 1990 the federal government was sufficiently confident in its university governance arrangements to impose them unchanged onto the East German system both in respect of Länder/institutional relationships and in the place of research in institutional missions and performance. Germany retains the most Humboldtian university system in Europe but has not been immune to state pressures: the wish to strengthen institutional leadership has led to the creation of university general boards (as in Portugal), and the evidence of international competition has led to the introduction by the Federal Ministry of the Exzellenzinitiative, which over time may transform previous assumptions about the equality of performance between institutions.

Like Portugal, Hungary has developed through many political vicissitudes but like Portugal it also retains many of the characteristics of its past structure. Subjected to communist rule for forty years controls over university research were transferred to an Academy of Science. The academy's powers and functions have now largely been returned to the universities themselves;

specialist single disciplinary institutions linked to ministries which had been encouraged under the Soviet pattern have been merged into larger and more comprehensive universities. With the fall of communism the system quickly reverted to its Humboldtian origins, as in other Central and East European systems. As a civil servant explained:

> We live by the Humboldtian model: this is how our institutions came about in principle after the 1990s but mainly in the 2000s when we went through a major network transformation. So the goal was to establish *universitas*-type institutions so as to unite many fragmented specialised institutions, urban-type institutions with more disciplines, because this tradition was [derived] from our large institutions like Eötvös Loránd University (formerly the University of Budapest). (8)

After a relatively brief period of a high level of operational autonomy and academic freedom during the 1990s and early 2000s, which was accompanied by increasing university deficits, government-level authority structures began to reassert themselves in 2014 in the imposition of non-academic administrators, the chancellors, to sit alongside rectors, but reporting directly to government and, in 2021, the appointment of a five-person politically appointed foundation board in twenty-one of twenty-seven public universities which have complete powers over institutional strategy and financial policy. In addition with the expulsion of the Central European University and interventions over some politically sensitive areas of research, governance has become much more top down and interventionist. Government has moved from being sympathetic to state steering from a distance to becoming an aggressive and interventionist reformer of the system imposing management solutions requiring universities to align themselves with national and regional priorities. However, while physical modernization has taken place in terms of infrastructure, new student residences and refurbished buildings, one interviewee suggested, before the 2021 changes, that 'the inner social structures, hierarchies, the functioning of the whole system didn't change at all' (9).

Perhaps the clearest evidence of the continuing influence of the Napoleonic and Humboldtian models has been in academic organization. While in the Anglophone model universities were always responsible for their own academic and financial management; even when they became fully funded through the UGC, they retained their previous operational independence. Indeed this was enhanced when they began to charge market rate tuition fees to international students. In the UK, therefore, universities always needed to have appropriately effective central governance and management structures to keep them out of deficit; 'shared governance' ensured that senates played a full part in operational matters with final decisions on financial matters taken by governing bodies. Faculties were academic coordinating bodies only, chiefly responsible for funnelling curriculum issues from academic departments through for the senate's approval. Historically, until recent reforms, a good many of the financial and managerial functions that were the normal responsibilities of UK universities were, in continental Europe, carried out by the state so that strong central institutional management was less necessary – rectors were elected and carried out primarily academic and ceremonial functions, and detailed academic decision-making and internal resource allocation were primarily located in faculties headed by elected deans. The balance was quite different to the UK's: the centre was weak and the faculties were strong; institutional autonomy mostly related in practice to freedom at the faculty level rather than to the powers exercised by the institution's central authorities.

In France a determined attempt has been made through legislation to reduce faculty powers without, however, much success; such an attempt in Germany would perhaps meet the same fate though the creation of university boards and the centralizing of budget decision-making represent attempts to strengthen the centre at the at the expense of the faculties. The same could be said of Norway, Hungary and Portugal: in Hungary a university with a spread of powerful faculties was described to us as 'a classic Humboldt-style structure' (10). What is apparent, in spite of widespread change at state governance and management level, is that a main legacy of the Napoleonic and Humboldtian models is the continued existence of a dominant academic faculty structure protecting academic interests which can restrict the powers of the rector and which, on occasion, can be an important factor in resisting or diluting externally imposed reform.

While it is possible to argue that the three main governance patterns established in the late eighteenth and nineteenth centuries still frame the governance of European higher education and that they remain deeply embedded in their state and university structures, it is also clear that their influence is weakening. Primarily this is because elements of the models no longer accord with the priorities of governments. But change has also been driven by wider pressures. Three events have been key. The first was the Lisbon Declaration of 2000 when the European Community committed itself to aim to become the most competitive and dynamic knowledge-based economy in the world and to raise expenditure on R&D in Europe, academic and industrial, to 3 per cent of GDP. These commitments have not been achieved but have had the effect of alerting governments and universities to the importance of university-based research and its relationship to the economy. The second was the publication of the Shanghai Jiao Tong World University rankings in 2003, which disclosed, in tables that bore the hallmarks of impartial and comprehensive research, how poorly some highly regarded European universities were ranked. This was a key factor in arousing university competitiveness within and outside Europe and provided the launch pad for the politically influential research by Aghion *et al.* (2010) which linked university governance structures with performance. The third driver was the Bologna Process initiated in 1999 which, by engaging the academic community in transformational cross-border curricular reform, also opened the minds of the participating academics to trends which, brought back home, rendered their universities more open to change (Voegtle, Knill and Dobbins 2011). In Portugal a dean commented that it brought 'the end of the scholastic approach [to teaching] in the university'. These events did not sweep historic legacies aside but they did prepare governments and universities for the interlocking trends of modernization which have characterized the last decade.

The 'modernization' of European systems: some comparisons

Germany

Germany represents a large higher education system with 93 public universities out of 399 higher education institutions. However, of 2.6 million students, 1.6 million are in the universities, about 50 per cent in the twenty-five largest universities. In research, ten universities secure about twice as many awards from the Deutsche Forschungsgemeinschaft (DFG), the state research body, as the average for the system as a whole. State control of higher education is shared between the Federal Ministry of Education and Research and the individual Länder to whom the governance and funding of their institutions are devolved. State authority is diffused between a number of interlocking bodies: the federal ministry, the ministries in each of the Länder, the DFG, the Wissenschaftsrat (the Science Council) and most importantly the Standing Conference of the Ministers of Education and Culture, which provides a close interface between federal and Länder interests. Teichler describes this network of bodies as operating in a continuous state of negotiation (Teichler 2018). One result is that the university system is protected to a significant extent from the personal intervention of a minister and decisions in respect to changes in governance policy are embodied in legislation which will have been the subject of close discussion between all relevant government bodies and the Conference of University Rectors. A very senior non-German working in the system commented: 'I always feel that in the German system it's especially important whether a decision is legitimate, whether you are allowed by a law [that you have] the position to take it' (11). Higher education is regulated by law not by ministerial decision:

> It's written in the Universities Act. We all act according to the ever-same constitutional law. What the freedom of research, teaching and the self-government of universities means has undergone changes in many Länder. That's what the law intends. (senior Länder official) (12)

The Law on the Freedom of Universities (*Hochschulfreiheitsgesezt*) in the North Rhine Westphalia Land signalled a significant step away from some traditional features in Land-university relationships. Step by step Länder governments used flexibility in approving regulatory change to reinforce procedural university autonomy, recommending that Länder forgo their previous role in appointing professors and Kanzlers to the institutions, funding universities through block grants rather than via line budgets and giving universities the right to enhance academic salaries in individual cases while continuing to keep the academic community on public service contracts. This did not eliminate Länder involvement from university governance, however, because they retained the right to prescribe the size and the make-up of university boards and to require an annual financial report to the Länder government.

Individual Länder had the ability to vary many of these arrangements, but Teichler (2018) suggests that in practice the resulting differentiation between Länder systems remains small when compared to differences between university systems across Europe. One important and universal consequence was the enhancement of the role of the rector and of an institution's executive group. This loosening of Länder's controls, particularly over finance, had consequences for institutional management as resource allocation between faculties and other heads of expenditure was now devolved to the institution:

> I think our university has gained autonomy compared to the past... in past years it was that appointments of professorships was on the table of the [Land] ministry and now the university has the power to do this, but on the other side with autonomy we also have the autonomy of our financial environment... [but] having this autonomy you have to make maybe also some decisions that are not so popular in one faculty because you have to support another faculty and you cannot support both faculties in a manner as in the past because you have not the resources that you had before. (university senate member) (13)

In other words, financial autonomy transferred decision-making power to a university's central authority to play a stronger role in the determination of priorities in the most sensitive of areas particularly when resources were being reduced.

Although there is general agreement in the academic community that the reforms have given universities greater autonomy, the presence of the Länder government cannot be discounted. At the technical level Länder continue to own university buildings, and although the federal government provides funding for building maintenance, the disposal or acquisition of new buildings requires approval from the local ministry; universities often continue to be tied in to Länder procurement procedures; one rector complained to us about 'micro-management' (14). More importantly a Länder government could exercise considerable informal influence, not based on any legal authority over university decision-taking. In one institution it was said:

> Money is a big problem for us and the less money you have the more dependent you are on the political government that they give something for something. This level of debt can buy decisions. (university senate member) (15)

At the same university an interviewee commented on how important it was to keep in touch with the Länder parliament and at another university a senior member of the university executive noted how frequent his meetings with the Länder ministry were. To achieve results, negotiation had often to take place. Such negotiation would not be determined unilaterally unless, as a senior state official confessed, 'we cannot come to an understanding'. He went on to say:

> These are the formal opportunities to exert influence. This way the parliament, as a budget legislator, gets the chance to block funds from the global budget [block grant] of the universities for certain projects... To me informal influence means that we talk to the universities and say 'we would like this' or 'could you do that?' or 'we would be willing to allocate funds for that'. (16)

On the other hand, close relationships could have positive effects for both sides. In many Länder their universities' research capacity in science and technology is seen as an important component of policies to attract industry or enhance the local economy. In one case the state authority wished to create a mini-technopolis and decided to 'leverage' (the word used explicitly by a senior Länder official (17)) its technical university by offering it a growth plan of an increase of about 20 per cent in student numbers and a budget increase of €20m over five years. In return it wanted to see the university more 'management-orientated' (18) and made it clear that it expected a new rector to be appointed from outside rather than inside the institution. Close liaison with the political authorities to draw up a complementary development plan was maintained by the chair of the university board, an experienced industrialist. This is an exceptional example where the politically perceived needs of the state coincided with the interests, as seen by some senior members of the university, but it also illustrates how in certain circumstances state governance may impact on institutional governance. One consequence in this case was pressure from within the university, successfully exercised, to include academic representation on the university board to improve the information flow between the board and the executive and the senate.

The federal ministry may appear to play only a coordinating role but in practice it is much greater; some voices, both in state ministries and in the universities, suggest its direct influence is growing. This is largely due to the introduction in 2005 of the Exzellenzinitiative which rewards a restricted number of universities at regular intervals for research excellence. Criticized by many inside the universities for being contrary to the spirit of homogeneity between institutions our interviews suggest it is having a profound influence not just on the level and concentration of research but on internal governance structures, the role of the rector and the authority of the executive group, to deliver convincing institutional research strategies. In many German universities budgets are distorted by the fact that they include substantial research funding from the DFG and other research sponsors, and indirectly benefit from their affiliations with the Max Planck Society, the Frauhofer Gesellschaft, the Leibniz Association and other sources of external funding, giving the impression of a generous funding regime, but these monies are awarded for limited periods only and are not available to fund university teaching. Universities are dependent for the latter funding on their Länder, on a federally funded Higher Education Pact of between 20 per cent and 25 per cent of their budgets and on limited term injections of federal funding for specific purposes.

German universities do not charge tuition fees either to home or EU students or to international students so they are almost entirely dependent on public funding, making them vulnerable to policy changes at government level. It is widely acknowledged that while project funding for research is well supported, universities are underfunded for their teaching function. One effect of the limited term funding programmes provided from the federal ministry is that they breed a climate of financial uncertainty in which universities are discouraged from awarding permanent academic appointments. An unfavourable interpretation of the federal ministry's approach to funding is that it is designed to enable the ministry to retain its ability to steer the system. However, whatever uncertainties this engenders the system remains essentially stable; universities work in closely integrated partnership with federal and state governments. According to a senior Lander official the system's governance is based on a 'network of relationships where the focus rests on coexistence in order to drive the universities forward' (19).

England

When the decentralization of higher education to Scotland and Wales took place in 1992, to be followed by full-scale devolution in 1998, and to Northern Ireland in 1999, the UK Parliament retained responsibility for higher education in England; the English system at 135 universities in 2019–20 was far larger than Scotland's 19 universities, Wales' 8 universities and Northern Ireland's 2. Devolution was not unqualified, however, as the UK government retained responsibility for policy and funding research across all four nations. Unlike Germany there is no stability in the state's machinery for governing the university system, a reflection perhaps on the priority which the government invests in it. In 1992 English higher education remained the responsibility of the Department of Education and Science (DES) but in 1995 the Research Councils, the major source of university-based research project funding, were removed to the Department of Trade and Industry (DTI). This department itself morphed into a new Department of Innovation, Universities and Skills (DIU), to which English higher education was itself then transferred from the DES. This department was then enlarged to become the Department for Business, Innovation and Skills (BIS) until in 2017 English higher education was shunted back to the Department for Education (DfE) leaving its research functions remaining in a Department for Business, Energy and Industrial Strategy (BEIS). This period of continuous reorganization could be interpreted as evidence of governments seeking the best structure to bring together higher education with its economic stakeholders; in practice what it illustrated was the low importance attributed to higher education in UK political life: in the turmoil of Brexit, and changes of Tory prime minister, no less than four Ministers of Higher Education held office within two years.

Perhaps the most destructive organizational change was the last, in 2017. In 1985 the University Grants Committee (UGC) embarked on its first Research Assessment Exercise (RAE), the forerunner of the German Exzellenzinitiative and the French IDEX, which reallocated the existing research element of UGC recurrent funding of institutions (the so-called Quality Research [QR] element) to reward performance. The RAE, later renamed the Research Excellence Framework (REF), remained a non-devolved national exercise carried out under the control of the Higher Education Funding Council for England (HEFCE) and its results have had a significant impact on the dynamics and structures of all four UK systems. Unlike in Germany, there was no principled objection in the UK to rewarding universities differentially according to research performance or to recognizing that some universities were research-intensive, while others were more teaching-orientated. The UK had always had universities like Oxford, Cambridge, Imperial College and University College, London which were particularly distinguished for research, and the RAE and the REF served only to extend the differentiation; already 75 per cent of national research funding was being awarded to only 25 per cent of the institutions. As far back as 1994 a group of research-intensive universities had formed themselves into the 'Russell Group' to distinguish their interests from the rest of the system. But the significance of the 2017 departmental reorganization was that the QR funding was detached from the higher education budget which was transferred back to the DfE and remained with BEIS. At the same time HEFCE was abolished with the strong implication that policies on research would be reached separately from policies about the education of students and that the interests of institutions and the interrelationships between teaching and research within institutions would become increasingly secondary to national control over research policy.

Meantime important changes were taking place in the funding of teaching. Since the mid-1980s financing the expansion of student numbers had become an acute problem especially in a country where the Treasury played such a dominant role in policy (Shattock 2016). As far back as 1980 the Thatcher government had compelled the introduction of full-cost tuition fees for international students (thus creating a tuition fee market in which universities were eager to compete to compensate for severe reductions in direct government funding) and in 2000 tuition fee charges of £1,000 were introduced for home students except in Scotland. These rose to up to £3,000 in 2006 and to the substitution of tuition fees of up to £9000 for public funding for teaching in 2010 coupled with the creation of a 30-year loan repayment scheme for students. Higher education was to be seen as a market: student numbers were uncapped from the controls previously operated by HEFCE, HEFCE itself was replaced by the Office for Students (OfS) whose main function was to act as a regulator only, and a 'level playing field' was claimed to be created to encourage entry to the market by privately funded institutions.

The political and economic motivations of the policy were outlined in a White Paper:

> Competition between providers in any market incentivises them to raise their game offering consumers a greater choice of more innovative and better quality products. Higher Education is no exception.
>
> (BIS 2016, para 7)

A civil servant responsible for the implementation of the 2016 White Paper compared the approach proposed to that of a regulated industry and a student's position to an 'energy bill payer'. The language of the OfS was, he said approvingly, much like that 'of regulated utilities' (Shattock and Horvath 2019 note 4 pp 33–34). An obvious and anticipated consequence of the application of market principles was that some institutions would flourish and others fail. The chair of the OfS offered no comfort to the latter:

> We expect universities to develop realistic plans for the future which reflect student demand for their courses and how they can meet that demand. Should a university or other higher education provider find themselves at risk of closure our role will be to protect students' interests and we will not hesitate to intervene to do so. We will not step in to prop up a failing provider.
>
> (Adams 2018)

Unsurprisingly the policy of 'competition and choice', as it is described by Willetts, the responsible minister (Willetts 2017, p. 277), has introduced a profound sense of instability to the system both at the top level of institutions and within them, where course leaders feel themselves at personal risk if recruitment targets are not met. This represents the antithesis of the German approach to the control and management of higher education: whereas German universities remain publicly funded, English universities are reliant on tuition fee income; while the German federal government and the state government see their role as protecting and advancing the interests of their institutions, the UK government sees the English system as a market where institutions may thrive or fail depending on their market strengths and irrespective of their particular academic contributions or their importance to the surrounding community.

The adoption of a policy of governance via the market has had important implications for institutional governance: decision-making power has seeped away from university senates and academic boards to vice chancellors' executive committees and to externally (lay) dominated governing bodies which increasingly act like company boards. Academic participation, once a special characteristic of UK university governance (Moodie and Eustace 1974), has been greatly reduced and has been almost wholly eliminated in some universities low in the reputational rankings; marketization of the system has pushed many universities into private sector style competition. The concept of the maintenance of a strong university system as distinct from strong individual institutions, such a feature of the German system, seems, in England, almost to have been abandoned.

Norway

A sharp contrast to the corporatization of English universities can be found in what one interviewee described as the 'very, very strong notion of publicness' in Norway, where the 'understanding of education and knowledge as a public good is very, very engrained in the system' (20). This is accompanied by a high degree of trust between the universities, the Ministry of Education and Research and the Norwegian Agency for Quality Assurance in Education (NOKUT). In practice the ministry has taken the leading role in the drive for Quality Reform, a programme initiated in legislation in 2003 but 'the way of policy-making... is very focussed on... a consensus orientation but also having a knowledge base into the decisions they [the Ministry] take' (21).

A key element of the Quality Reform was to improve the organizational and management capability of institutions to match up to the demands of greater autonomy. In the UK, at a comparable point, the government supported recommendations that the vice chancellor should be designated as the 'chief executive' of the university and that encouragement should be given to external (lay) boards of governors to 'assert' themselves over the wishes of an academic senate (CVCP, the Jarratt Report, 1985). In Norway, however, the ministry offered the universities two models; a continuation of the existing system where the rector was elected by the staff of the institution and became automatically chair of the general board but with the difference that a director of administration would be appointed to handle all administrative matters creating in effect a dual leadership, or an alternative where the rector was appointed by the board for a limited term but was given full academic and administrative powers. In these latter circumstances one of the external members would take over the chairmanship of the board and there was no requirement for the appointment of a director of administration. The majority of universities opted for the second model; the ministry accepted their choices.

Universities make annual reports to the ministry and every year receive a visitation from the Ministry armed with centrally constructed data about their performance. This in many circumstances would be regarded as a demonstration of ministry power but the Norwegian reaction is pragmatic: 'we see all the results and the kind of expectations they have for the next period' (22) not, 'this is an imposed infringement of our autonomy'. Partly this is because university autonomy and university self-government were adopted by the ministry as the key strategic method of achieving greater accountability and outcome results but it also reflects a Nordic 'idea that higher education is part of society, that it frames it… [and that] in a way it's part of the Nordic welfare state' (23). If an institution's performance did not match the indicators looked for by the ministry, the case would be referred to the Norwegian Agency for Quality Assurance (NOKUT) which would agree with the institution a programme to bring about improvements.

An important dimension of higher education policy relates to regions. In Norway 'regional politics is always important; it's a really important sort of underlying argument in everything else' (24). In the past the Norwegian system was dominated by classical research-intensive universities in the main population centres and colleges, and mostly primarily teaching institutions located in the regions. As part of the Quality Reform the government took the view both on grounds of quality and for reasons similar to those reflected in Germany's principle of 'homogeneous living conditions' that the college system should be upgraded to a university system based on institutions that, in accordance with Humboldtian principles, were research active and that this should be achieved through institutional mergers designed to strengthen their academic base. The result has been a reduction in the number of institutions, but not of campuses. Consonant with its consensual approach the ministry invited colleges to make proposals for mergers rather than deciding itself on the structure it wished to achieve and NOKUT was given the power to control the process in approving the academic viability of colleges joining forces. If merged colleges could satisfy the quality evaluators that they had at least four doctoral programmes of an adequate strength and five masters programmes in different areas, NOKUT was empowered to recommend the conferment of full university status. Carrying through such a major process of restructuring represents confirmation of the effectiveness of the approach but also reflects a broad consensus about the way higher education policy should develop across political parties.

Stability of financial support has played a large part in the success of the Quality Reform programme. Norwegian higher education is approximately 90 per cent funded by the state and, even though a modest reduction of 0.5 per cent in the unit of resource is applied each year, the financial pressures felt in many other European countries have passed the universities by. Universities are owned by the state; tuition fees are not chargeable either to home or to international students. Funding for institutions is based on historic costs so that there is some differentiation between the long-established universities like Oslo and Bergen and the newer institutions; zero budgeting has not been applied but 60 per cent per cent of the resources allocated is linked to student numbers, 15 per cent represents a component for research and 25 per cent for teaching. In addition research project applications are generously funded through the Norwegian Research Council (RCN) to the benefit of the research-intensive universities. Norway is a small system with nine public universities, nine specialized universities (three private) and twenty-three university colleges but has accomplished a major restructuring aimed at improving quality, increasing research, widening access and attracting more international students. This is a significant achievement which offers compelling models to Wales and Scotland as they chart their devolved and, in Scotland's case, would-be independence, from their much larger English neighbour.

Wales

The governance of higher education in Wales has important similarities with that of Norway: the system is small by the standards of England or Germany with only eight universities; the government's style of operation is comparable to Norway's – 'the tradition in Wales is to seek consensus wherever possible' (senior official in the Welsh Government) (25); the comparable need to re-shape the system to the geophysical character of the country imposes a requirement to promote institutional rationalization. Where they are not similar is that the Welsh economy operates at 25 per cent below the EU GDP average, while Norway's is 48 per cent above. Post-devolution the country finds itself with too many and too small higher education institutions and, by closures of campuses and mergers, has reduced its number of universities from thirteen to eight. Its higher education system remains heavily interlocked with England: 27 per cent of Welsh domiciled students enter English universities and 56 per cent of students in Welsh universities come from England. This is an important factor in forcing Wales, reluctantly, to follow the English tuition fee policy. It is often argued that the original decision to decentralize Welsh higher education from the UK system was made politically on the back of the decision to decentralize control of Scottish higher education but this would be to underestimate the distinctiveness of the Welsh system. The original Welsh colleges, founded in the nineteenth century and grouped under the federal University of Wales, owed their origins to concerns about lack of educational opportunities in Wales for a largely working-class population and a key feature of the Welsh Assembly Labour Government's policy, post-devolution, was a reflection of past historical attitudes: 'poverty alleviation, tackling poverty and doing what could be done to widen access, widen participation, encourage people from disadvantaged backgrounds into higher education' (senior official in the Welsh government) (26). A second distinctive feature was the existence of the Welsh language, which is now extended into becoming an alternative to teaching in English across Welsh higher education.

But the governance of Welsh higher education is different to England in other ways. The first is the relationship between the institutions and the government. As one governing body chair reported:

> The feeling in the government in Wales is that they have this direct contact with individual institutions and with individuals in those institutions so that [his vice chancellor]… has this one-to-one contact with [the Minister for Education] and with other ministers and [the First Minister] himself.

They have this direct contact, direct challenge from Wales to Cardiff [University] as the Russell Group university to set an example to the rest of the higher education sector, and you don't see that in England at all with a 140 or so institutions: the link between a particular vice-chancellor and the government in Westminster is as tenuous as he or she wants it to be. (27)

A second difference is that Wales has retained an intermediary body, the Higher Education Funding Council for Wales (HEFCW), to be replaced by a new Tertiary Education and Research Commission, which stands between the government and the institutions and which undertakes visitations to Welsh universities, as does the Ministry in Norway, although more on a consultative rather than the inspectorial basis that would be found in Norway. A third difference is that the Welsh government's philosophical position is essentially anti-market, and so, although forced to adopt a tuition fee policy very close to that practised in England, it remains hostile to a core principle of UK government policy. And finally, the Welsh Assembly has backed its own principles in referring in policy documents to the public good, a concept implicitly rejected in English higher education documents, and has taken steps to establish a tertiary, as opposed to a higher, education system. In this new system, and as part of the rationalization of institutions referred to above, strategic decisions have been taken to incorporate further education colleges into university structures both to improve widening participation in areas of economic deprivation and to integrate the impact that higher and further education can make on the economy of the area. In prospect, this is the most radical plan to utilize higher education institutions to address economic agendas in deprived areas that has been adopted in the UK.

As in Norway the Welsh government has sought to engage the institutions fully in decisions over mergers, although the mailed fist has occasionally been seen to exist beneath the velvet glove. Nevertheless one institution, the Cardiff Metropolitan University, itself the product of previous college mergers, resisted merger proposals put forward by the then minister and has so far been able to pursue a robustly independent course. As in Norway, mergers may have been achieved without rancour at senior institutional governance bodies, although that has not always been the case within the institutions themselves. Nevertheless, this is the only successful programme of mergers that has been accomplished in the UK.

Scotland

It is a matter of history that Scotland's higher education has developed much more independently of England than has Wales. Its four 'Ancient' universities (Edinburgh, Glasgow, Aberdeen and St Andrews) all have their origins in the Middle Ages, played a significant role in the Scottish Enlightenment and were beacons of scholarship in the nineteenth century long before the English provincial colleges in cities like Manchester, Leeds and Sheffield were upgraded to university status. Scotland developed its own school system and a tradition of four-year rather than three-year first degrees, so that cross-overs between English and Scots students at the first-degree level were very much less than between England and Wales. Although the Scottish National Party (SNP), the majority political party in Scotland, lost the Referendum for Independence in 2014, the country voted strongly to remain in the EU in the Brexit Referendum and continues to press for a second referendum on national independence. A senior Scottish official in interview said of Scotland: 'it's not because we want to be different, it just is different, and it's [that is, English higher education] got decreasing relevance to how we see things up here' (quoted in Shattock and Horvath 2019, note 11, p. 52).

It is not necessary, therefore, to argue the distinctiveness of Scotland within the UK and its higher education system is testimony to the differences: in 1992 the Scottish government insisted that the Scottish Central Institutions (the polytechnic equivalents in Scotland) which were granted university status along with the English polytechnics should be research-active and rejected the idea current in England that some universities should be regarded as 'teaching-only' institutions; Scottish universities rejected the English approach to quality assurance which concentrated on the achievement or maintenance of standards and, in conjunction with the Quality Assurance Agency, re-wrote its protocols to emphasize quality enhancement. Finally, from the moment when Alex Salmond the then first minister of the Scottish government declared 'the rocks will melt with the sun before I will allow tuition fees to be imposed on Scotland's students' (quoted in Riddell, Weston and Minty 2016) it was apparent that a parting of the ways was occurring between Scottish and English higher education policy. The principle set out in the Scottish National Party's (SNP) election manifesto that 'access to education should be based on the ability to learn not the ability to pay' (Scottish Government 2007) draws a sharp line between a traditional Scottish approach and the increasing policy of marketization being adopted in England.

The SNP has been in power in the Scottish Parliament since 2007. It is more socialist and more outwardly nationalist than the government in Wales and has sought to pursue a social and economic policy more aggressively through the university system than anything attempted in Wales. It inherited, but has reluctantly retained, a Scottish Funding Council (SFC) as an intermediary body, although it attempted, but was defeated in the Scottish Parliament, to make the Council subordinate to a Scottish National Enterprise Board, which by implication would have had the effect of linking universities primarily to a national economic agenda. It imposed, however, a regime requiring universities to complete Outcome Agreements, renewable every three years, showing how they had implemented priorities outlined in letters of guidance from the minister. Reports, to be signed off by the university governing bodies, were demanded annually and were required to include very detailed information against widening participation, social and economic targets. This monitoring exercise has the potential to impinge seriously on institutional autonomy but, perhaps through the influence of the Funding Council, has not yet done so.

The government has, however, intervened directly through legislation to amend universities' governing structures to make them more 'democratic'. This has involved making the chair of the governing body a position subject to institutional election, requiring two representatives of trades unions to be appointed additionally to the lay membership and the addition of more student and staff members. The Act was passed in the teeth of the combined opposition of the universities.

A feature of the governance of higher education in Scotland is the particular texture of the relationship between the universities and the government. Scotland has nineteen universities which span famous international research universities like Edinburgh, whose budget is only 20 per cent directly dependent on the Scottish government recurrent grant, and relatively small primarily regional institutions like the University of the Highlands and Islands, which is 80 per cent dependent on government funding. Through their representative body, Universities Scotland, the universities work closely together to hold the government to account over its funding policies to maintain the international status of Scottish universities and to resist incursions into institutional autonomy. However, as compared to England it is a small system and personal relationships between senior university figures, heads of institutions and chairs of governing bodies and members of the government are inevitable and welcomed:

> And that obviously has two sides, the closeness of government has a good side. The good side is that we have immediate access to government, we don't have to go through junior ministers or civil servants, we speak directly to the First Minister or Deputy First Minister or they pick up the phone and speak to us.
>
> (senior university figure quoted in Shattock and Horvath 2019, note 19, p. 57)

But, as the speaker continued, the negative side is consistent references to the government's social and economic objectives and to priorities in the Outcome Agreements. These conversations can be a good deal less congenial than they generally appeared to be in Wales.

The largest area of friction undoubtedly surrounds funding. The universities, and particularly the research-intensive universities, are concerned to maintain parity with comparable universities in England, if only for the sake of their international ranking. The lack of tuition-fee income from Scottish students obviously places a considerable burden on the government, which requires the kind of strict student number controls now abandoned in England. In 2008 Scottish universities reached an agreement with the government that parity of funding with England would be retained and on their part they would commit themselves to a closer alignment to the government's objectives. But over the years backsliding in respect to funding levels has certainly occurred. The state's budget is clearly stretched to match the levels of income of some English universities and even with the levels of international tuition-fee income which can be commanded by universities like Edinburgh, Universities Scotland are pledged to continue to press for maintenance of financial parity with universities in England with whom they are in direct competition for research council and REF funding. Whereas in Wales, with only a single Russell Group university in Cardiff, the Welsh government sees maintaining that university's international standing as a matter of national importance, the

Scottish government has a more onerous task in reconciling its principles and policies with the size of its purse.

Hungary

Kovatz, Heldrich and Chandler (2017) identify four stages in the development of the governance of Hungarian higher education: from 1946 to 1985 the imposition of a Soviet system; from 1985 to 1998 the restoration of the Humboldtian model and an increase in institutional autonomy; from 1998 to 2011 a transition period where steps have been taken through institutional mergers, many of them forced, to create a unitary from an essentially binary system of universities and colleges; and from 2011 where new legislation has created a turning point characterized by the adoption of a more centralized and government-controlled approach and decreases in institutional autonomy. We could add a fifth stage with the government's offer of transfer to foundation status indicating the intention to make them more self-financing, while establishing management boards which override the role of the senate or the rector and a significant number of whose members are drawn from Fidesz the leading political party. Unlike the situation in Germany and Norway our interviews threw up evidence of profound academic dissatisfaction with the current regime: 'Hungarian higher education is a landlord system, it's a funded system. Everyone has a small territory and depends on someone' (28); higher education in Hungary is characterized by 'a combination of a neo-liberal system [which is] nationalistic state controlled' (28). Both statements were made before the transformation to foundation status. They reflect even then the rapid changes that had occurred in Hungarian politics and in the management of the higher education system which, in the process of making legitimate adjustments consequent on joining the EU, has moved to becoming directly interventionist. Hungary's Constitution, amended in 2013, reads:

> Higher Education institutions shall be autonomous in terms of the context and methods of research and teaching; their organisation shall be regulated by an Act. The Government shall, within the framework of an Act lay down the rules governing the management of public higher education institutions and shall supervise their management.
>
> (Article X, para 3 quoted in Kovatz, Heldrich and Chandler *op cit*)

This leaves ample authority to legitimize the extensive government intervention that has taken place.

This should not be allowed to distract, however, from the reform task which confronted the government in the post-communist era. In addition to establishing colleges in rural areas the Soviet model had encouraged the creation of a number of specialist disciplinary institutions and in the immediate aftermath a significant number of private colleges emerged. Between the mid-1990s to 2016 the number of higher education institutions had been reduced from eighty-nine to sixty-four, of which twenty-seven are public-sector higher education institutions. Even this number might seem surprisingly high if comparison is made with, for example, Sweden, where a population of 10 million, the same size as Hungary, is served by only fourteen public universities and seventeen colleges. A feature of the Hungarian system is that a concentration of 45 per cent of its students study in Budapest, primarily at Eotvos Lorand University (ELTE), formerly the University of Budapest.

Higher education is the responsibility of the Ministry of Innovation and Technology. Within the ministry there is a state secretary, whose responsibilities are largely functional: a useful advocate of the universities' interests in higher levels of decision-making but not a policymaking post. As in Norway the state retains ownership of university property. A major problem of the last decade has been resources – in a decade when student numbers have fallen by 26 per cent, funding levels are only at 2008 levels (EUA 2020), a prime reason for universities to grasp the 'dowry' which accompanied the invitation to foundation status. In a system where directly or indirectly institutions receive over 80 per cent of their funding from the state, this has led to significant political and management pressures. This has been addressed in a number of ways. One of these has been in relation to tuition fees. Tuition fees were introduced in 1996, remission being linked to performance in the university entrance examination. Initially over 90 per cent of students entered the system as state-funded; the proportion has since decreased to 65 per cent. Since performance in the university entrance examination is a key factor in state support, the full fee-paying students tend to be concentrated in the less prestigious universities. A second issue was that universities had a persistent debt problem. Recurrent grants to institutions were based largely on historic figures and were allocated on the basis of student numbers per academic discipline. Before the transfer to foundation status the elected rector received 20 per cent for the administration of the university, but except for a small development fund, the allocation of which was the responsibility of the senate, the remainder was automatically directed to the elected deans to allocate according to local priorities within their faculty. As a professor explained:

> The financial arrangement is very much linked to the size of the faculty. And this is a fight between the big ones and the small ones… it is like a tribal fight. (30)

But the problem lay less with the senate:

> The faculties are completely independent, they operate absolutely independently … the university budget does not dare to interfere with the faculties… virtually every decision is made at faculty level. (academic at a major university) (31)

The speaker went on to name the faculties in his university which were in his words 'bankrupt'. Since universities were part of the public service, the state, for political as well as for social and educational reasons, could not allow universities to go bankrupt so efforts were made, both through cross-subsidies within the universities or through strategic hand-outs in the form of special grants from government, to eliminate the problem. Indebtedness, however, simply re-emerged the following year. The situation encouraged extensive lobbying of ministers, not only by rectors but also by deans in respect to their faculties. As one senior administrator described the situation:

> Everyone knew that something has to be changed and one of the clearest reflections of this was the continuing increase in debt. There was mistrust on the part of government towards the whole of higher education but the depth at which each university was [in debt], however, varied widely. (32)

Universities had always had directors of finance (directors general of the economy) who reported to the rector but whose appointment had, in fact, to be approved by a minister, but the government went much further by creating through legislation the post of chancellor who would report not to the rector but to the ministry and who would, organizationally, sit alongside the rector with the power to veto a rectorial decision on financial grounds and to control expenditure right across the university. Appointment to the post required approval by the prime minister. This was a draconian step and, by any standards, an affront to university autonomy, reducing the rector's role to academic decision-making alone, with the chancellor able to intervene over any decision at any level in the university that had financial implications. It goes without saying that the reform was deeply resented by the academic community, and while in practice conflicts were mostly avoided by rectors and chancellors finding ways of working together, the imposition of an official of this standing reporting direct to the government exposed the fragility of institutional autonomy when the state chooses to act arbitrarily.

But the problem of weak university central governance and the situation in which rectors could be out-voted in their senates over resource allocation issues remained, and in 2021 the government passed legislation to entrench a lay-dominated board, one of whose members is the chancellor, to take full command of management, strategy and finance. The rationale as stated by a member of the government was that: 'The universities are somewhat limited by the state household rules. Our universities should apply the same financial rules as… [the private sector]' (33). But this seriously understates the purposes and effects of the legislation. It is true that foundation status frees universities from overcontrolling government bureaucracy – for example foundation universities can now carry year-end savings forward to the next year rather than have to return all but 10 per cent to the government and are able to take full control of their property assets – but the most significant aspect of the legislation is to require boards to direct universities' strategy to be aligned to the purposes of the state and to invest them with managerial powers of implementation presumably primarily under the aegis of the chancellors (34). The effect is to further weaken the role of the rector, which is to remain an elective office, and effectively to eliminate the role of the academic community from institutional strategy policy formulation. The 2022 re-election of the Orban government entrenches the new system for many years to come.

Thus a modernization which could have been interpreted as essentially the reinforcement of a policy to bring university finance under control in practice becomes a policy to subordinate academic autonomy to the needs of the state. There may indeed be further darker political and ideological implications. In a radio interview a week after the legislation was passed, Prime Minister Victor Orban made it clear that no 'internationalist-globalist' members would be appointed to the boards and that universities which were important for national sovereignty and self consciousness should not 'become some kind of globalist institutions that lose theirnational character' (Radio Kossuth interview on 30 April 2021 – from minutes 17.33 to 17.37). The decision to appoint active politicians to permanent positions on the new boards might seem to confirm that the control of something more than finance is in mind.

Any assessment of the governance of the university system in Hungary in the recent past must take account of the fact that the formal structures and the legislation were more porous than in other comparator countries. This was because of both the extent of private communication between rectors, chancellors and ministers and the use of special tendering processes to solve particular institutional financial problems. It is too early to say whether the most recent reforms will bring order back into university finance or what the effect will be in forcing an alignment with national and regional policies, but it is difficult to believe that the imposed political solution which this represents will provide the last word in the 'modernization' of the governance of Hungarian higher education.

Portugal

Just as Hungary can be characterized as a 'Middle European' country, Portugal is keen to represent itself as 'Southern European'. As in Norway and Hungary, geography exercises an important influence on its university system with the older universities (Lisbon, Porto and Coimbra) concentrated in the centres of population on the coast and the polytechnics/applied sciences universities located in the agricultural hinterland. A dominant characteristic of our interviews was the sense of the degree of change, not all of it welcome, which the system had been through since the end of the Salazar regime and the democratizing of the universities. Student participation had risen from 15 per cent of the twenty-year-old age group at the time of the Revolution to nearly 35 per cent in 2010 to 50 per cent in 2020 without compensating increases in government support so that funding levels were comparable to funding levels per student in secondary education. The international economic downturn in 2008 had hit Portugal particularly hard and academic salaries were cut by 25 per cent and remain low as compared to other European countries.

Bureaucracy, much of it related to increasing state control, was increasing. As one senior academic at one of the older and most prestigious universities said:

> I think the University [has] changed a lot. When I entered university my feeling was that we were in a space of total freedom... if we did our work and our own research and we publish and we [give our] classes... we had the space and flexibility to do more or less what we want.... Now research is not anymore an individual work, we must be integrated in teams and work within research lines and groups and we have coordinators and a lot of bureaucracy, and even teaching changed a lot; we implemented Bologna in 2007 and... 10 years ago we didn't have an Accreditation agency or evaluation agency so we used to direct our programmes in a more informal way, and now we need to present results to be evaluated and assessment [has] to be integrated in a lot of formal structures. In that sense it changed very, very much. (35)

With the fall of the Salazar regime the higher education system became part of what Neave and Amaral describe as the 'emancipation from traditional society and, at the same time an emancipation from a regime and its ideology that were inseparably associated with the past' (2012, p. 25). There followed a period of collegial self-government and a move towards a state supervisory model guided by the Conference of University Rectors. This culminated in the University Autonomy Act of 1986 and parallel but more limited autonomy legislation in 1990. At one level the legislation guaranteed university autonomy. A senior university official explained:

> It's important to understand the high degree of autonomy that universities have. Universities are not under the supervision of the government, they are under the authority of the government. That means the government cannot set a strategic course for every university, it's up to the university to decide for itself its structure. (36)

But the actual position is less positive. Heavily influenced by developments elsewhere in Europe such as the launch of the European Association for Quality Assurance (ENQA), the government established an accreditation committee which on a first review exercise rejected over a 1,000 programmes and imposed a regular six-year cycle of programme reviews. New undergraduate programmes can only be approved within that period unless an existing programme is discontinued and can only be continued if, after two years, they can be shown to recruit an intake of twenty students. No new masters or doctoral programmes can be offered without approval by the committee which is also empowered to deny approval on the grounds of national priorities or of duplication of programmes offered by other universities. Criticism of the bureaucracy involved is widespread.

Another area of heavy European influence was research. Even now there is little competition between Portuguese universities in research (evidence suggested that there was little, if any, staff mobility between institutions and that incentives to move, as you would expect to find in a competitive system, were minimal) and an acceptance exists that Porto and Lisbon Universities will be dominant in attracting the best qualified students as well as being the two leading research universities (they rank 301–400 and 401–500 respectively in the Shanghai Jiao Tong table). In order to catch up with the rest of Europe and because of the recognized weakness in research, the Ministry of Education and Science and the National Foundation of Science and Technology encouraged setting up joint research centres between partner universities. To encourage collaboration these centres were often located away from main university campuses and this together with the creation of joint governance arrangements gave them a focus and an independence from their central university authorities. Before long the Ministry and the Council began corresponding directly with the research centre directors and not through their institutions about long-term research agendas, research grants and postgraduate programmes so that the most successful centres became semi-autonomous creating, as one senior academic described, 'resentment on the side of the rectors because they feel they are powerless in that regard' (37). As machinery to develop a national research profile, this has been a successful innovation but the separation has not helped the creation of university research cultures and has weakened the exercise of autonomy through the universities' own structures of governance.

In principle the development of quasi-independent research centres would seem to conflict with the decision to offer universities foundation status, technically described as acting as a public foundation under private law. This was intended to guarantee operational as well as substantive autonomy, to strengthen the powers of the rector and introduce a board which included external (lay) members. Originally recommended by an

OECD report the new measure was enacted in 2007 and was reinforced by the decision in 2010 to fund universities on a four-year contractual basis though the funding levels have only in 2019 climbed back to the level in 2010. This had the effect, after the budget reductions of 2008, of bringing greater financial stability to institutional management. The universities remained heavily dependent on state funding, however, and although tuition fees were charged, they remained at what were described as a 'very, very low' level (38). An important element in the decision to opt for foundation status was the transfer of property assets from the state to institutions and the ability of institutions, subject to some government controls, to borrow funding for investment purposes. But maintaining the substance of institutional autonomy has been difficult. On the positive side a senior academic and director of a research centre said:

> I think [we have] come a long way… a vivid illustration of that is that nowadays when there is a problem in the institution, especially in the main universities, they will say 'how shall we solve this?' They do not say 'we need to ask the government for more money'. (39)

On the other hand, it is difficult in a country suffering financial stress which has an authoritarian tradition to safeguard institutional autonomy convincingly at a national level and without recourse to intrusive regulation, and this translates itself downward into the management of the bureaucracy at an institutional level where staff 'tended to resort a lot towards control and control of processes because that's where they felt more comfortable' (40). As one external member of a general board, in a university that did not opt for foundation status, put it:

> We as a public university are completely autonomous in financial terms, in pedagogical scientific terms, we are autonomous from the government. [But] of course we have to comply with all the rules and regulations. (41)

The university system has undergone a transformation since the end of the Salazar regime and academic cultures have been fully revived, particularly in research, in spite of the most serious financial pressures, but it is threatened by an overload of bureaucracy which appears to be endemic to the operational modes of the state.

The strengthening role of the state

The changing involvement of the state

However much tradition frames the development of higher education systems, their governance is affected by contemporary changes in context, most noticeably in the last decade by the twin factors of a growth in student numbers in most countries and by the downturn of the European economy. One or both of these pressures have dictated change in all the national systems studied, raising a host of issues: system enlargement and rationalization, the management of austerity, the continuing viability of publicly funding universities (often a shorthand for whether to introduce tuition fees), accountability to states sceptical about the financial and academic implications of massification and the organizational issues deriving from states' growing interest in developing a research policy distinct from policy about the education of students. The impact of the Bologna Process and the calls for 'modernization' by the EU Commission re-emphasized the role of the state in system change. How states have dealt with these pressures has depended on relations with their higher education system, the stability of the system itself and the political, economic and cultural context of the country.

The issues surrounding student numbers have offered some of the greatest pressures. Here we see that in the richer countries the expansion of the 1990s has continued: between 2008 and 2018 German numbers increased by 45 per cent, Norway by 29 per cent, England by 10 per cent and France by 18 per cent (with only Italy showing a fall in numbers of 8 per cent) (EUA 2020). In all these countries (except Italy) the problem has been for governments to expand their resourcing in line with the numbers at a time of acute internal competition for resourcing other parts of the public sector of the economy. In Portugal, while the expansion has been slower, the issues have been compounded by the drift of numbers away from institutions in the rural areas to the older and more prestigious institutions in the major cities at a time when a weak economy was struck by the universal downturn in 2008. In Hungary the position is different again with a fall of 26 per cent in numbers between 2008 and 2018, a situation it shares with other post-communist countries (Czech Republic, Poland, Romania, Slovakia and the three Baltic states (EUA 2020). The impact of these changes had significant effects on institutions. For example, in the UK, and taking a rather longer time frame, whereas in 1992 only two universities exceeded 20,000 students, by 2018 the figure had risen to forty; universities like LMU Munich (39,000), Oslo (27,000), Lisbon (47,000), Porto (31,000) and Eötvös Loránd (28,500) in spite of the overall decline in numbers in Hungary) became mega-institutions. Size not only became an important factor in their governance structures but also made the institutions more difficult to reform from the outside and for the state to introduce policy change. Conversely when numbers decline it invites state intervention to produce mergers and creates cut-throat student recruitment competition between institutions to maintain viability; valuable collaboration between urban and provincially based institutions becomes more difficult to sustain.

Expansion has raised questions of public accountability and, in systems which are directly publicly funded, offers grounds for policy interventions by the state; all governments have sought to reinforce state control over their higher education systems. One step has been to change funding mechanisms to reward institutional performance; another has been to try to make universities more 'business-like' in their management, in practice giving more management authority to rectors and vice chancellors; a third has been to introduce external (lay) membership into institutional governance through lay or part-lay boards (or in the UK to give existing lay boards greater authority); while a fourth has been to impose accreditation or quality mechanisms designed to reassure the state or the public of the educational value of the academic product which institutions were offering. There has also been an emphasis on institutional autonomy but often in the expectation that greater autonomy would enhance their contribution to the state's objectives whether fiscal security, research performance or a strengthening of the system. In this, governments have followed different strategies: in Germany and Norway, for example, giving universities greater autonomy, in England, creating a market designed to reinforce the performance of some institutions and to expose the weakness of others, in France, rationalizing an unwieldy structure, in Italy encouraging institutions to greater operational effectiveness and in Hungary and Portugal to tighten bureaucratic control. The evidence suggests that the role of the state in higher education is growing in all European countries.

Institutional autonomy

It has become a commonplace of European higher education policy to work towards the concept of the state steering autonomous institutions. No European state would fail to endorse the legitimacy and desirability of university autonomy (although Hungary's constitution, quoted above, and the latest reforms come very close to doing so) yet in practice state steering is becoming more directive. In Germany there is evidence, and not just from the impact of the Exzellenzinitiative, that the federal government is imposing more pressure on the Länder. In England a radical market-orientated funding mechanism has been imposed; in Norway the Quality Reform programme has driven change, while in Hungary and Portugal after periods of relaxed relationships, governments are reasserting control. In Scotland the SNP government has ambitions to extend its powers to direct the system, but is opposed by a united universities' front. In Norway, Wales, Hungary and Portugal this has been accompanied by system-wide rationalization, institutional mergers and the upgrading of colleges to university status. (In Norway and Wales, while undertaken with the encouragement of the state, mergers were essentially based on voluntary decisions by the institutions; this was not the case in Hungary.) Universally, reform programmes are being driven top down not bottom up.

In most countries reform programmes are implemented through legislative action and changes in regulations. This is especially true in Germany, where the governance of the system is essentially controlled by regulation and civil law. Historically, this would have contrasted strongly with the Anglophone more hands-on approach through an intermediary body except that the English switch to governance via the market required 158 pages of new regulations to be attached to the legislation abolishing the Higher Education Funding Council. Subsequent events suggest that the Higher Education and Research Act of 2017 and the new Regulatory Framework which it launched are pushing England much closer to Germany and other European countries in determining system management by law rather than by custom and tradition. In England, Shattock and Horvath (2019) find that institutions have retained operational autonomy but have lost substantive autonomy. (The decision in Scotland to impose annually updated Outcome Agreements represents a good example of this in another system.) In some systems governments still retain the ownership of capital assets and therefore circumscribe institutional freedoms to manage their property portfolio to the best advantage of their academic programmes. In others, universities are tied into public sector procurement programmes which impose bureaucracy and delay on the acquisition of quite trivial articles of equipment. Two countries, Hungary and Portugal, have sought to encourage internal institutional reform by freeing universities from some elements of government control by permitting institutions to become 'private' foundations. The Portuguese experience does not suggest that this necessarily achieves all that was anticipated unless the state exercises a self-denying ordinance not to impose fresh bureaucratic restrictions on institutional freedoms. In Hungary it appears to be more a device to exercise government control by another route.

However, in only two cases in the last decade have governments stepped in to impose amendments to university constitutions: in Scotland, where the SNP government passed legislation aiming to 'democratise' university governing bodies, and in Hungary, where the government intervened to impose chancellors, appointed by the prime minister, with powers to veto decisions by the rector as a way of bringing institutional finances under control and followed it up by imposing a new constitutional structure, foundation status, on a significant part of the university system. In Scotland the legislation was opposed by the universities which are now finding ways to adjust to it. In Hungary the introduction of the chancellors struck at the heart of institutional autonomy providing all too clear an indication of the state's willingness to override universities' machinery for self-government. The continuing issue of institutional debt was understandably a matter of government concern but the state's action was minatory and smacked of exasperation, an arbitrary act, rather than a considered reform. However, the follow-up legislation to transfer universities into public service foundations marks a clearly long considered step to cut back institutional autonomy and make the higher education system more subservient to the politically determined interests of the state.

The growing separation of research from teaching

An essential element of the Humboldtian model was the concept of the close engagement of university teaching with research. This was epitomized in the German system but was also the norm in the Anglophone model though in practice in the UK after 1992 when the polytechnics and the Scottish Central Institutions became universities the assumed allocation of staff academic time as 50:50 research and teaching became impossible to substantiate across the whole system. In Germany the continued existence of the Fachhochschulen served to preserve the research-orientated mission of the university sector, whereas in the UK it became defined increasingly by the results of the RAE/REF. But in both countries, and across Europe in general, the recognition of the importance of research to national economic prosperity brought changes in the way governments managed higher education. In the UK the government has opted for the most extreme position of separating policy and funding for research, including the operation and funding of the REF, entirely from the funding of teaching, locating them in two separate ministries, the BEIS Department and the DfE. This has left the powerful research and innovation committee within BEIS with the ability to make decisive policy impacts on the higher education system, for instance, the institutional effects of research concentration, regional policies, the effect on academic career development and subject spread, with no balancing implications for the system particularly in respect to funding. In Germany, although the federal ministry covers both education and research, policy originates from two separate departments: education is a devolved responsibility of the Länder, while research is led by the German Research Council in Berlin and by the powerful research agencies, the Max Planck Society, the Frauhofer Gesellschaft, the Leibnitz Association and others. The Research Council also supports research infrastructure, buildings and laboratories as well as sponsoring the Exczellenzinitiative. The result has been that recurrent funding has moved away from basic support for education and research towards competitively based funding through the Research Council which, as described above, has left universities structurally underfunded and reliant on research funding to balance their books. As a consequence research priorities have gained over teaching and funding per student has fallen. While the attitude of one senior university official that 'research is the trademark of a university whereas teaching is rather more for technical colleges' (42) may not be typical of views across the system, there would probably be very little disagreement with a senior Länder administrator's view that 'That the core problem [in Germany] is the structural neglect of teaching... the conditions of reputation and success are all just research focussed right down to the individual career'. (43)

Norway and Portugal follow Germany in linking responsibility for education and research in single ministries, and both link their forward plans for the development of research with the 2000 EU Declaration's aim to raise expenditure on R&D to 3 per cent of national GDP. Neither country has sought to reinforce research by adopting high-profile university research evaluation exercises as the UK and Germany have done, and as France and Italy have also done. France and Portugal present the most individualistic approaches to prioritizing research: France with its tradition of concentrating research development through a central research agency, now the National Research Agency (ANR), has sought to invigorate university research away from its previous model through the *Loi pour la recherché et l'innovation* in 2006 and IDEX in 2010; Portugal with its historically low research base has established a National Foundation for Science and Technology (NFST), which carries out six yearly assessments of university research. In Portugal, the NFST has encouraged the creation of interuniversity research groups which provide a critical mass of researchers. ('Nowadays as a freelancer in research you don't have a chance in Portugal even if you are very good' professor in technological field (44).) The ministry has two divisions, one devoted to university and polytechnic funding and the other to research. In the period 2005 to 2011 great efforts were made to establish research as a viable activity:

> Science was always a sort of prince charming and the education part and the funding of higher education institutions was always less protected than science. (senior academic) (45)

In other words there was always the temptation within government to divert resources towards research. One result, as described above, was to build up large interuniversity research centres on sites away from the individual institutions over which the NFST could exercise direct influence rather than indirectly through the universities themselves. The government plans to double its public expenditure on R&D over the next decade to meet the Lisbon target with the likely effect of prioritizing research over teaching needs yet further.

Hungary may intend to follow similar policies but has shown little sign of wanting to put similar government machinery in place. Research and innovation are located in the portfolio of the Ministry for Innovation and Technology, but in practice the driver for research is a separate National Research, Development and Innovation Office (NRDIO), which answers directly to the prime minister. A recent EU review found that the NRDIO had 'a poor evaluation culture' and concluded that 'the public research system is underfunded and it is also fragmented across a number of universities, institutes of the Hungarian Academy of Sciences and sectoral institutes supervised by different ministries' (European Commission 2016, pp. 11–12), a structure looking essentially unchanged from the era of Soviet dominance. Steps have now been taken to distribute Academy institutes among universities but from a research perspective this only represents the first stage in the assimilation of centrally managed research organizations into university research cultures. Hungary continues the shared difficulties of other Central and East European countries; in 2016 only Romania, Bulgaria, Cyprus and Malta were below it in a ranking of proportionate GDP spend on R&D in the EU.

The conclusion to be drawn from these accounts is that increasingly policies towards research and education are drawing apart even when they are retained in the same ministry. In such cases they form separate departments and research is in the position to be a powerful bidder for national resources. At one end of the spectrum we have the UK, where research and education are formally separated in different government departments, while on the other we have Portugal, where the National Foundation for Science and Technology has encouraged a situation where research is in danger of being divorced spatially as well as culturally from its parent universities, and Germany, where the research agenda, and the funding support for it, is driven by powerful research agencies operating outside the control of a university's central authorities. It could be said that national policies are converging for reasons of reputation, positioning in ranking tables and pressure from the EU. But the consequences of this for higher education's teaching function and the historic belief in the integration of teaching and research are far reaching.

System management

A marked contrast exists between the management of large and small higher education systems. In the large, relationships between institutions and the state machinery tend to be impersonal and governed by regulation or by well-understood custom and practice. In Germany, for example, legal authority is a determinant of action; while relations between universities and state governments may be close and politically rewarding, there is no evidence that this translates into direct *ex gratia* financial support. In England (and, effectively, in Scotland and Wales) the tradition has been governance through custom and practice (arbitrated through the Higher Education Funding Councils), but the move to adopt the market as the driver of system management has led to the introduction of a formidable regulatory regime. The position in the smaller countries is rather different. The situation in Scotland and Wales is protected by the continued existence of intermediary bodies. But in Portugal and Hungary a considerable political element in decision-making is apparent. In Portugal a former minister said:

> My own experience is this, you need to have a very good understanding and a good articulation and good dialogue between the minister responsible for higher education and the prime minister because the prime minister in a certain way is the one that leads the process. The ministry of finance, the minister of finance, is always a very powerful element within government but within certain limits the prime minister is the key person on what should be allocated to higher education. (46)

Unless there was a special policy initiative there is no reason to suppose that a UK prime minister would ever have become personally involved in the allocation of a budget to higher education. The single exception to this was in 2001 when Tony Blair was convinced over dinner at Downing Street by a group of senior vice chancellors that English higher education was underfunded, which led to the increase of tuition fees from £1,000 to up to £3,000. On the other hand, in Portugal a rector could claim that he used his personal friendship with the prime minister to solve problems and added that 'all the rectors can phone the minister directly to solve things' (47) so that this was not his exclusive privilege. Ministers themselves have personal networks which reach into universities and encourage communication outside the formal framework of university-state relations. In Hungary, this intimacy between universities and the government seemed to shade into something even more informal. As an example the chair of one university governing body, interviewed before the most recent reforms, described how:

> If there is an issue that the university would like to solve, general resources or finance then we either write a letter or I personally go and talk to the minister or whoever is in charge of that part of higher education. That happens… in cases of pushing for giving the money, sometimes not who should be appointed but that the appointment should be speeded up. (48)

A former rector, however, also interviewed before the most recent reforms, condemned what he saw as a deterioration in state governance:

> These changes have made good room for buddy-buddy deals. So, for example, if you have a good time with the ministry you can simply visit the minister and convince him what I am doing is great and you get extra resources and then the university system is used to channel the money. (49)

In small countries where no intermediary body exists between institutions and the government, it is difficult for rectors not to seek to engage ministers and even prime ministers in their problems especially when they have long-standing social and even academic links with them. The dangers implicit in the undermining of funding systems or the exercise of special influence are obvious. Norway, in its commitment to consensus, consultation and evaluation, seems to have found a way of avoiding them. A good example of the Norwegian government's way of doing things can be seen from the following:

> The Ministry suggested at some point maybe we should look into the ownership of institutions, make institutions sort of self-forming… corporations which are self-owning private entities [that is, offer them foundation status as in Portugal and Hungary, above]. Uproar came quickly and the Ministry said OK well if you don't want it we don't do it. (50)

This quotation reveals two aspects of the governance of Norwegian higher education: the first that Norwegian institutions felt that they did not need to augment the autonomy they already possessed as part of a public service by choosing foundation status and, second, that the ministry was responsive to consultation with the sector as partners in a common endeavour. What

Norway has – and German universities with their Länder governments – is a close relationship based on bureaucratic understandings which command mutual respect following widespread consultation. Such relationships take time to build.

Trust

Norway exhibits, to a greater extent even than Germany, a degree of mutual respect and trust between the state and the university system. No other system would permit without protest an annual review visitation of institutions by ministry officers based on detailed but shared data. (Scotland maintains a regular institutional visitation programme but it is carried out by the Scottish Funding Council and does not have governmental involvement.) In both Norway and Germany one encounters a sense of common purpose between universities and the state. This is by no means the case in England or in Hungary. In England, Universities UK (UUK), the representative body of vice chancellors, can best be described as an advocate body rather than as adviser to government as most rectors' conferences in continental Europe would perhaps see themselves. In part this is political – the academic community in England is not happy with the marketization of the system, on which it was not consulted, and a very substantial majority of academics voted against leaving the European Union, the political priority of the Tory government – but in part it reflects concern over the way the state conducts itself, the absence of consultation and the extent to which policy change appears to be based not on quantifiable evidence but on a neoliberal mistrust of the traditional values that universities felt were embedded in the system. In Hungary the state is in a hurry to catch up with the rest of Europe but is acting in an arbitrary manner with little attempt to consult the university system as to ways and means. Its concern about university deficits and the lack of machinery to deal with the problem was understandable but the imposition of chancellors reporting separately to the government created a precedent for state intervention into university governance which will be difficult to erase.

One measure of the extent to which the state trusts institutions can be seen in the powers of their national accreditation machineries. In the UK an accreditation body has never been envisaged since historically the award of a university title automatically conferred the power to award degrees. More recently the Quality Assurance Agency (QAA) has been empowered to make a grant of degree-awarding powers a staging point in an institution's application for full university status. In extreme circumstances degree-awarding could be revoked by the OfS on the recommendation of the QAA. A similar situation exists in Germany and Norway, where universities are self-accrediting; in Norway NOKUT, however, operates an extensive evaluation and information service. In Hungary and Portugal accreditation is a power reserved to the state. In both countries, post-Bologna, national accreditation exercises were carried out to remove programmes perceived to be sub-standard, and in each case review periods were established (Hungary five years, Portugal six) thus ensuring that the state had a continued role in supervising the quality of university qualifications. In Hungary, however, the accreditation committee has not been funded at a level to make five-year national review possible and at the bachelor level it would appear that the provision has lapsed except in the case of new programmes. In Portugal the six-year review remains in force reinforced by the regulation that new programmes will only be approved if it can be demonstrated that an equivalent number of programmes are withdrawn. In both countries accreditation is required for the introduction of new masters and doctoral programmes. These restrictions both reflect the two states' concerns to match up to European standards in the post-Bologna age but also emphasize the degree to which governments wish to continue to exercise direct control over their university systems and do not feel able to allow them to exercise full academic autonomy.

2

Institutional Diversification, Regional Disparities and System Management

Nothing illustrates more clearly the diversity of European higher education both in back history and in state policies than the steps different countries have made to respond to the pressures of massification and the need to address issues relating to regional economies and to inequalities of provision. Here the larger countries with the more extensive systems of higher education – the UK, Germany and France – were first in the field in the 1960s and provided models, or at least possible comparators, for the smaller nations to draw on as their systems expanded. The consequential reforms in structures created path-dependent programmes of development which over half a century later still provide key elements in policy discourse. Diversity in geophysical characteristics and in population concentrations contributed significantly to the approaches to system management that were adopted. Political history too played its part: the fact that Portugal was recovering from a forty-year dictatorship and Hungary from a similar period of communist rule meant that their attempts to modernize to align themselves with other EU nations imposed a dynamic which was not present in the larger countries whose reform programmes, while punctuated with legislative and other changes, were more incremental in their development. The fact of Hungary and Portugal joining the EU and participating in the Bologna Process was much more significant for them and other smaller systems of higher education than for the larger well-developed systems. The result is that while the structures can look much the same, the underlying drivers of the systems can be very different: the evidence points to a much more differentiated set of systems than might appear on the surface.

Binary lines

Germany, the UK and France, as the three largest and most developed university systems, were the first to have to encounter the demographic pressures of the post-war generation and the demand for curricula more adapted to the needs of a post-war industrial economy. This included expanding existing institutions, creating new ones, upgrading technical and teacher training colleges and licensing the growth of private colleges and universities, including those run for profit, to absorb the increased numbers. A key policy issue was whether to protect the existing public universities and their research mission by spreading the expansion over non-university institutions as well as the universities and establishing a clear separation between them creating what became known as a 'binary line' between what were viewed as first-tier and second-tier institutions. The distinction that was drawn was based on the historic research mission of the universities on the one hand and the more vocational curricula and different subject base of the non-universities on the other. The pattern was also adopted widely in the smaller systems like Hungary, Norway and Portugal, and elsewhere in Europe. However, in every country where a binary line was established it later came under challenge on the grounds of the perceived inequality of the structures in which institutions that were carrying out teaching responsibilities comparable to those in universities, that is to first-degree level, were accorded a lower academic status. In particular, they were not funded for research even though such institutions could be seen as being more relevant to the labour market than the existing universities and, in some countries, to regional economic needs. The different approaches to working through the issues raised by the existence of binary lines represent a key differentiating factor between higher education systems.

At the same time governments were also facing demands to reinforce their economies with new technological institutions specially designed to reinforce their technical labour focus and to strengthen industry. The same policy issues arose: should this take place based in the university sector, which were usually more associated with study in the pure sciences rather than in technology, or outside them and what influence did this have on the qualifications of the students and the status of the institutions? would the new institutions compete with the existing universities for research funding? Germany, the

UK and France resolved these issues each in their own way. Thus Germany opted for the most *dirigiste* solution, namely to protect the historic integrity of the university system, albeit reinforcing it with ten wholly new university foundations, but creating in the late 1960s and early 1970s a new system of vocational, technologically based institutions, the Fachhochschulen, which taught primarily applied disciplines but were not given the right to award doctorates, by this means delineating a clear binary distinction from the universities. Some half a century later there are now over 200 Fachhochschulen and the distinction between the sector and the ninety-three public universities remains largely unchanged with the research mission firmly embedded in the universities. The university remains dominant in terms of student numbers although the proportion of students in the Fachhochschulen has increased from 27 per cent in 2002 to 38 per cent in 2020.

Policy development was much more diffuse in the UK. In a period of eleven years between 1956 and 1967, the UK in effect transformed its system, first creating a new category of higher education institution outside the long-established university system, the Colleges of Advanced Technology (CATs). These were distinctive in that they were responsible initially to their local authorities not to central government and in that they awarded a higher diploma under the auspices of a new national awards body rather than a degree. In 1963, as a result of a recommendation by the Robbins Committee, which had been appointed by the government to chart the development of higher education up to the early 1980s (Committee on Higher Education, Report 1963), the CATs were upgraded to the status of technological universities, removed from local authority control and brought under the University Grants Committee (UGC); their three-year diplomas were converted into degrees.

Four years later, however, with a change of government, a third category of institution was created, the polytechnics (which were paralleled by the establishment of new Central Institutions in Scotland) formed by multiple mergers of technical colleges. These were also placed firmly under local authority control; they were to award degrees through a new Council for National Academic Awards (CNAA), but were to be local and anti-elitist. A leading advocate of the new institutions coined the title 'the People's Universities' for them, indicating that social and political studies carried equal weight to technological or professional studies as the main drivers for the creation of the new sector (Robinson 1968). By 1985, with university growth restricted, the polytechnic sector had grown to be as large as the university sector. This had not been the Robbins plan: while seven new universities were established as a first step towards meeting the expansion prior to the report's publication, the report had envisaged student numbers being concentrated in the existing universities, as in Germany, with the prospect of a limited number of technical colleges being perhaps upgraded to university status only towards the end of the period up to 1980. The new polytechnics and Scottish Central Institutions were envisaged as teaching institutions and not funded for research although they were, unlike the Fachhochschulen, given the power to award doctorates through the CNAA. In 1992, however, they were made universities, thus removing the binary line. This created a unitary structure except that the former polytechnics and Central Institutions, had only a modest record of research and were deprived, *de facto* if not *de jure*, of the ability to compete on a level-playing field for research monies with the pre-1992 universities, a situation reinforced by the outcomes of the research assessment exercise (later the Research Excellence Framework, REF) first introduced in 1985–6. Thirty years later the impact of the abandoned binary line can still be seen in UK higher education in the dominance of the pre-1992 universities in research and in the institutional status which that confers. This informal reputational ranking has been replicated in respect to a third generation of colleges, the colleges of higher education, which have since been upgraded to university status (the post-post-1992 universities). Many, unfairly, still carry the reputation of being teaching-only universities.

In many ways the French system has charted a middle course between the German and the UK approaches: it has never had an explicit binary line, and like Germany, it simply expanded its university system to accommodate the expansion of student numbers. But in 1966 it responded to the post-war pressure for specialist vocational/technological institutions in a different way by creating a new institutional model the Instituts Universitaires de Technologie (IUTs), which, instead of being self standing institutions as in Germany, or surrogate universities, as in the UK, were attached to existing universities, where they remain to this day, awarding two-year diplomas as well as three-year degrees and undertaking research. This was an altogether more carefully considered model than the CATs in the UK, founded a decade earlier, were established with an eye to traditional regional disparities in student access as well as to acting as a motor for wider regional development. In the UK, the universities had historically established themselves in centres of population which, apart from in the Southwest and the North of Scotland, were fairly well distributed across the country. When the polytechnics and Scottish Central Institutions were created they were based around existing technical institutions that had themselves grown up as local authority colleges also in urban environments. This had the effect of siting many of them in close proximity to long-established universities which served to emphasize the disparities between the two sectors.

The situation was very different in Norway, Hungary and Portugal where regional economic disparities, regional demographics and the dominance of a small number of historically prosperous metropolises played a major part in policy development. In Portugal, a senior academic made the point that 'the country is very much concentrated on the coastline in a few cities on a strip of land. And this is where all the main universities are, so from Coimbra, Porto and Lisbon, and that's it' (4); a former education minister explained that the result was that 'we have 60 per cent of our students concentrated in two large cities, Lisbon and Porto, and say 45 per cent of the research in Lisbon so Lisbon is a large concentration followed by Porto' (5). But non-research institutions could have other roles: a senior academic praised his institution for establishing a campus in an area of depopulation to serve as an 'anchor' aimed at 'producing professionals, highly qualified professionals… the majority of them focussed in the main interests of this region' (6); or the example of Braganza – 'Braganza is now a city which lives essentially out of its polytechnic… the city has 45,000 inhabitants and 10,000 are students and out of these 30 per cent are foreign students and have completely changed Braganza' (7). Holding students in the rural areas, strengthening rural economies and diversifying the system lie at the heart of the government's policy of founding of new institutions or merging polytechnics to form universities away from the historic urban centres imposing an additional geophysical differentiation between regionally based institutions and those positioned in major areas of population: a professor of forestry spoke of being at 'a so-called small university in the countryside' (8), while another, a professor of agronomy, talked about being in 'a small university town,… a municipality, a relatively small municipality… [which had] some energy and then some dynamism' (9). A former minister described the situation:

> So for the hinterland... the population is very scarce and these institutions are anchors for people and for their regions so that they support a large number of activities in the area. And the number of students is important for towns. You have one town with 35,000 people and in the polytechnic you have 6,000 so it's very significant, particularly because they are the younger generation. (10)

These institutions have, in effect, become part of the infrastructure designed to rebalance the economy away from the established centres of population, commerce and industry. But in spite of the optimism of the staff they have a constant difficulty in meeting their student number targets in the face of the continuing drift of young people to the cities. Although research is concentrated in the Universities of Lisbon and Porto, the government has done its best to encourage it in these new institutions particularly in fields appropriate to their environment, forestry, crop production, viticulture and so forth. The establishment of joint university research centres, referred to in Chapters 1 and 3, represents a deliberate attempt to draw them into research as well as building on the strengths of the two kinds of institutions.

The Hungarian system shares many of the characteristics of the Portuguese but here there is only one historically dominant university, Eötvös Loránd University (ELTE), founded in the seventeenth century with its fourteen faculties located on three campuses in the heart of Budapest, the capital city. By contrast Pécs University, created in 2000, is situated in the most economically undeveloped region in the country and although one of the largest universities with ten faculties is actually spread over separate campuses, reflecting past mergers, distributed across the city. Although a senior member of the Pécs staff described the university as playing 'the role of the saviour of the region' (11), the mood in Hungary is generally more pessimistic than in Portugal. Both countries have ageing populations, but whereas Portugal has kept its numbers up by increasing its participation rates, Hungary has seen a student number decrease of 26 per cent in the last decade. ELTE, in Budapest, has maintained its numbers but Deprecen, Hungary's oldest university, has suffered a fall of 10 per cent; more extensive reductions have occurred in some regional institutions. It is not surprising that staff morale is low:

> In certain regions you don't have any problem [but] in other regions it is almost hopeless and the quality of teaching and learning is lower although the facilities, the infrastructure and the funding… [is]… the same. (former academic, now consultant) (12)

In a 2017 Report, the OECD commented that 'The influence of socio-economic background and school location (urban vs local) on educational performance is one of the highest in the EU' (OECD 2017, p. 23). A further factor are the widespread criticisms of the interventionist character of the state 'constantly directing the whole thing somewhere, what to do, how to do it' (13); in an underfunded situation, this discourages institutional initiative and enterprise that could be of economic benefit to regional communities.

The academic gap between first-tier and second-tier institutions is much greater in Hungary than in Portugal. Although after the Bologna reforms Hungary adopted the European pattern of a centralized structure of state control, the two sectors have remained far apart. The polytechnics were permitted to use the title of universities of applied science but not to award doctorates; their curricula remain unreformed and their student non-completion rates are one of the highest in Europe (OECD 2017).

Norway offers many contrasts to Portugal and Hungary. In the first place its GDP is much higher and higher education is better funded. The ministry makes an allocation against a notional student number figure and, quoting a well-placed university administrator, 'for about 50 years we have been given more and more' (14). In the second, Norwegian higher education policy, even more than in Portugal's, has a regional dimension which is founded on the principle, like Germany's commitment to homogeneity of provision, of 'a system that is present in all parts of the country' (15). But, like Portugal and Hungary, Norway has historic research universities in major cities (Oslo, Bergen and Trondheim) which dominate a system which includes a university in Tromsoe, founded in the north in the 1960s explicitly to counteract the loss of students to Oslo in the south, and a substantial group of universities of applied science, university colleges, and specialist colleges distributed across regions in the centre and the north of the country. Unlike

Hungary, and to a greater extent than Portugal, Norway has a commitment to making the provision of education in its rural areas comparable to what is found in the main centres of population and sees higher education as a universal public good:

> The idea that higher education is part of the society, that it frames it sort of, sounds very sort of fluffy and beautiful in a way, but in a way it's part of the Nordic welfare state. (senior researcher) (16)

Again, unlike Hungary and Portugal, Norway has a parliamentary political party, the Centre Party, whose programme is based on the equalization of rural to metropolitan provision, but in practice, there is a political consensus on higher education policy. This is evidenced by the fact that it was a conservative party which launched the Quality Reform process in 2000–1 (St.meld, nr 2000–2001) which, while addressing issues of governance and efficiency in the system, was effective in rationalizing the system from ninety-eight institutions, most of them very small, of which only four were full universities, to a situation where there were ten universities and twenty-three university colleges now calling themselves universities of applied science. The winnowing process was achieved through an extensive programme of voluntary mergers where individual campuses in small- and medium-sized communities were preserved in larger institutional units. A new funding system was introduced which adopted a common formula and criteria for all higher education institutions so that the regional institutions were encouraged to be research-active and to offer student: staff ratios comparable to the major universities. The formula was based on student numbers so that, as in Hungary and Portugal, institutions have become subject to issues arising out of demographic changes and student drop-out rates. This has created competition between institutions for students so that a quasi market now exists even in a system where tuition is free. Some campuses face serious shortfalls which raise difficult governance and management questions about institutional viability and potential conflicts over the principle of equity in provision across rural areas.

The higher education systems in Wales and Scotland share many of the issues which in their different ways characterize Hungary, Norway and Portugal. Before the decentralization of UK higher education in 1992 (and devolution in

1998), Welsh and Scottish higher education were fully integrated with England in the UK system. After 1992, English higher education continued to develop as if it was still a UK-wide system but Wales and Scotland faced changed political issues and government requirements to align themselves much more closely with regional needs. Both, for example, found themselves answerable to very different political regimes than before and in both cases geophysical, economic and social issues, not previously prioritized in the centralized UK system, became of much greater importance. Both had 'second tiers' of former polytechnics or polytechnic equivalents, the Scottish Central Institutions, as well as other higher education institutions which called for assimilation into unitary systems alongside long established university sectors; the steps taken compare interestingly with those followed in these smaller systems in continental Europe.

In Wales, overprovision in the number of institutions required rationalization. As in Hungary and Norway a merger policy was adopted which reduced the number of universities from thirteen to eight. Unlike Hungary, however, and much more like Norway, these mergers were voluntary, though closely steered by the Welsh government. (One merger candidate, the Cardiff Metropolitan University, previously the Cardiff Institute of Higher Education, itself the product of the merger of four colleges, resisted all the merger proposals and became an independent university now with 11,000 students.) As in other countries these institutions are multi campus: the University of South Wales, for example, has four widely separate campuses and one of these has three separate sites; like Pecs in Hungary it has become a large university of over 23,000 students. To illustrate another parallel, this time with Norway, in another multi-campus merger in Wales it is admitted that one campus has been preserved primarily because its closure would have crippled the small town in which it is located. One other similarity is that in Cardiff University, Wales has a single large dominant university located in the capital city, with a research budget equal to the research budgets of all the other universities combined, making its position in the Welsh system comparable in many ways to the position of ELTE in Hungary. Where Wales is most unlike Hungary, however, is in its political culture which strongly favours consensus over direction and where heads of universities can expect national policy to be formed only after face to face dialogues with the responsible minister. The success of this approach can be seen in the establishment of an explicit tertiary education system where further education colleges have been informally linked to universities in order to extend the provision of higher education into areas of economic disadvantage, an initiative which could never have been implemented in the previous centralized UK system.

In Scotland, the university sector was more balanced than in Wales with its spread of nineteen universities, four of them with mediaeval origins and two of them (Edinburgh and Glasgow) in the Russell Group but a solid group of pre- and post-1992 institutions which have not needed to engage in mergers to confirm their viability. Scotland's governing political party, the Scottish National Party (SNP), is also very different to that in Wales and has strongly interventionist inclinations but for the most part these have been resisted robustly by a united university sector organization, Universities Scotland. However, where Scotland has a resemblance to Norway is in the similar need to bring higher education opportunities to a sparsely populated rural area, the Highlands, a mountainous region covering one-sixth of the UK's landmass, and to discourage the outward migration of young people to the more prosperous southern Scottish cities. Here the government has supported the foundation of the Highlands and Islands University, based in Inverness, which incorporates thirteen further education colleges and specialist research institutes in the north of Scotland and, using distance learning techniques, provides higher education up to and including doctoral level to remote communities like the Isle of Skye, the Orkneys and the Outer Hebrides. (The University provides the UK's only representative in the Association of Arctic Universities.)

A distinctive feature of both Welsh and Scottish cultures is an historical respect and particular support for education and the role of higher education in widening opportunities for learning. Both countries have maintained intermediary bodies, the successors to the previous UK funding councils, which provide a 'buffer' between the governments and the universities; in Scotland, the Scottish Funding Council has played a major role in defending the system against more extreme demands for universities to maximize their regional economic roles. In both countries, higher education is more closely engaged with government than is the case in England and commands more popular support.

Reshaping binary systems

The extent to which governments sought to shape the development of their higher education systems, and particularly the erosion of binary to unitary systems, varied greatly. Germany, as we have seen, essentially retained its binary structure by channelling student expansion to a considerable extent into its university sector while maintaining a growing Fachhochschul sector. The UK, on the other hand, once it had taken the decision to remove its binary line and create a unitary system, did not concern itself over the system's shape and left the ambitions for university status of the next level of non-university institutions, the colleges of higher education, to be reviewed and, in effect, approved or rejected by the UK Quality Assurance Agency (QAA) acting on academic not regional criteria. The QAA did not concern itself with system strategy or encouraging or discouraging mergers with the result that a new generation of universities came to be established in population centres, in smaller towns like Cheltenham, Chester and Chichester, which had previously missed out on hosting a university or a polytechnic but which had nurtured institutions with a primary interest in teacher training.

As it happened, however, these colleges, when upgraded to university status, introduced a new concept into English higher education, that of the 'anchor' institution, similar to examples in Portugal. In the economic downturn from 2008 when both local authorities and local industry suffered severe economies the new and continuously expanding post-post-1992 universities found themselves to be increasingly important players in their local and regional economies. (Shopkeepers protested when one such university proposed to close one of its branch campuses and withdraw students entirely from the town.) Often they became the town's largest employer and the only one to be introducing new lines of development; their staff and student expenditure helped to keep parts of their local retail market open; they became, in effect, 'anchors' of the local economy. This new role has added a new dimension to higher education policy and new responsibilities onto the institutions involved; community partnerships have become a much greater priority. Being an anchor university is adding a new descriptive category of university in England.

Norway, in line with its much more formal commitment to regional provision and to achieving consensus, encouraged mergers by offering a modest financial incentive but took the position that the initiative should rest with the colleges to establish institutional partners and merger strategies, subject only to confirmation by NOKUT. The process was thus intentionally bottom up. The consequence was the creation of multiple campus institutions sometimes extended over very wide geographical areas. But a key motivation was the economic value of the campuses to their communities and the opportunities they extended to students for access to higher education who for financial or social reasons chose not to seek admission to one of the historic research universities in the major cities. Such was the government's commitment to regional policy that in one case where an institution sought to close a campus located in a community of only 1,800 people on grounds of financial sustainability, it was suggested in parliament that the minister intervene to keep the campus open even though the regionally based governing body of the merged institution, to which autonomous powers of governance had been granted, had decided to close it (17).

Hungary approached these kinds of decisions in a much more top-down institutionally focused way. It inherited a Soviet-style distribution of 'second-tier' institutions linking mono-disciplinary institutions with individual ministries which, in the years following 2000, it redistributed by forced mergers to create comprehensive universities using ELTE as a model. This was succeeded by some further voluntary mergers, but from 2010 it de-merged some of the original merged institutions either to return them to their original mono-disciplinary situation (e.g. returning the Agricultural University back to the Ministry of Agriculture) or to merge them in some new formulation (Kovatz *et al.* 2017). Although a structure has been established where institutions can now themselves initiate bids for university status, the financial pressures led the chair of one 'second-tier' institutional governing body to conclude: 'I feel that every year it's simply a struggle for survival and there's no long term strategy' (18). In the meantime, the government adopted a new approach to university-state relations by establishing Corvinus University, created out of a merger between the Budapest University of Economics and the College of Public Administration, to be an institution which operated under privatized foundation regulations. According to a senior representative of the university, one rationale for the change was that:

> Since the state is the market outlet, the state says, being literally its owner,… and since the Hungarian public service is controlled by the Prime Minister's Office… the owners' rights are just, as in the life of a company, placed in the hands of the Prime Minister. (19)

In practice, the prime minister transferred his 'rights' to the minister but the statement raised questions about university autonomy: How far would this autonomy actually stretch? Is this simply a way of creating an alternative to the chancellor system or was a wider regime of state control foreshadowed? As a business/public administration university Corvinus University might have been too *sui generis* for such an experiment but within three years the government had legislated for the creation of foundation status for the whole system.

The contrast between the bottom-up process of closing the binary gap in Portugal and the top-down approach adopted in Hungary is considerable and is reflected in the way the institutions have developed and governed themselves in the two countries. In Portugal, the process was much more incremental and self-generative. Polytechnics were created in the 1980s by the government but sponsored by regional authorities and were formed by mergers of vocational and professional colleges in fields such as agriculture, forestry, engineering, accountancy, nursing and teacher training for primary schools. Their focus was regional, not national, and their students were primarily local. The outcomes of the Bologna Process offered both encouragement and systematization to the fifteen publically funded polytechnics because it regularized the award of three-year degrees and introduced the prospect of two-year master's degrees. Legislation was introduced which imposed a common form of institutional governance, less liberal than for the universities, but in practice very similar to the managerial structures laid down for the UK polytechnics. From this situation a number of polytechnics were later granted formal university status. The development of one such university, the University of Trás os Montes e Alto Douro (UTAD) in Vila Real, the capital of the Vila Real District in Northern Portugal with a population of 50,000, can be regarded as typical. Beginning in 1973 as the Vila Real Polytechnic Institute, on the initiative of its region, a college was established, initially to teach plant, animal and forest production. In 1978, it was upgraded to university institute status and in 1986 it became a university. (UTAD was never a nationally appointed polytechnic.) Since it became a university, although its range of disciplines and its student numbers have grown considerably, it was still possible for a senior professor to say:

> Our mission is very focussed on the importance of producing highly qualified professionals, the majority of them focussed in the main interests of the region, trying to be a kind of anchor to the people that leave as well [as those who] come here. (20)

Vila Real, like other parts of Portugal situated away from the coastal areas, suffers from depopulation both because of the fall in the birth rate and the seepage to Lisbon and Porto, raising significant questions about the viability of some disciplines in the university (already forestry can only be taught as a master's degree programme). Higher education is now managed as a unitary system; institutions are expected to be research-active and the joint university research centre approach, described in Chapter 1, has been effective in engaging the research interests of staff in institutions like UTAD. The Portuguese approach shows that an incremental process which continues to root its second-tier institutions in their regions within a unitary structure holds the possibility of moving the whole system forward without the institutional tensions that can accompany top-down government intervention and direction.

Diversity amongst institutions and in system architectures

The way governments approached the unwinding of binary lines and the reversion to unitary higher education systems tells us a great deal about system architectures in the different countries. In the UK, for example, after the blanket transfer of the polytechnics and Scottish Central Institutions to full university status, the process of integration was eased in Scotland and Wales by bringing all the institutions of higher education under devolved funding councils. In both countries the pre- and the post-1992 universities soon found ways of working together, but in England tensions stemming from the former binary system and from competition over student recruitment remained and are arguably still apparent today. After 1992, the upgrading of colleges to university status proceeded individually and incrementally under the aegis of the QAA rather than directly by the government itself and the outcomes were more easily assimilated.

In Norway, the assessment for upgrading to university status was from the beginning of the Quality Reform programme carried out by NOKUT, but here a bureaucratic qualification was introduced that regional colleges had to have four approved doctoral programmes in different fields and five master's programmes before becoming self-accrediting universities. Since the approval of each individual programme was subject to NOKUT accreditation and approval, the effect was not very different from the role of the QAA in the UK. However, the highly consensual approach to institutional mergers adopted in Norway may contain the seeds of future difficulties. A senior university administrator commented:

> In my opinion the university colleges did not really have a strategy, they did not really manage their own activities. They just grew because they were getting more money and more places and there were a lot of people who wanted to become a student. So they just opened their doors… and they just grew… it was not a strategy. (21)

The stability of the system is also affected by the scale of the mergers and the resulting organizational adjustments. Thus the new South Eastern University has, after a series of mergers spread over a decade, finished up with eight campuses, before securing university status. Structured now into four faculties, coordination is a challenge with faculties themselves spread over more than one campus and with campuses having different institutional and disciplinary cultures. As an institution with a 60 per cent student drop-out rate and subject to the continued draw of Oslo, it is vulnerable to potential changes in funding regimes but to consider the closure of uneconomic campuses would be to draw public and internal criticisms of policies which, it would be argued, smack of centralization or the abandonment of rural communities.

In Hungary, the character of the post-binary system is different because of the top-down nature of the government's approach but the problems implicit in managing merged institutions are not dissimilar. Thus the University of

Pécs, now an institution of some 30,000 students, began as the Janus Pannonius University, itself formed by a merger with the College of Pedagogy and the Technical College in Pécs and the Illyes Gyula College in Szekszard, but in 2000 it merged with all the other higher education institutions in Pécs to form the present university structure. A former rector described it even now as 'actually a loose conglomerate of ten small universities and faculties and it was tremendously difficult to achieve unification' (22). Facing shortfalls in home student recruitment, it has begun a campaign to attract international students which, it is said, has changed 'the mood' of the city.

> The fact that you see a construction site in Pécs, and we see a lot of them, it's all because of internationalisation. It has activated the private equity market, so they build apartment houses, which is good because it provides a good environment for students. (23)

Portugal is different again because it did not have the spread of colleges that were present in Norway and Hungary and the question of mergers did not arise in the same way; polytechnics were based largely on single institutions and their growth was determined by local student recruitment. Where Portugal encouraged inter-institutional activity, short of merger, has been, as we have seen above, at the research level with the establishment of joint research centres, often sited away from the participating institutions and inevitably beginning to establish a significant institutional independence from them. Longer term their continuing relationship with their sponsoring institutions represents a significant policy issue, but for the moment it offers a solution to a second major determinant of system architecture, the research divide. Here the differentiation between the larger and the smaller higher education systems is particularly marked.

The system where this differentiation is most apparent is the UK, where the frequent iterations of research evaluation processes since 1986 have produced an institutional research hierarchy which has structured itself from the Russell Group of research-intensive universities to institutional groupings like Million Plus and Guild HE, both made up exclusively of post-1992 and post-post-1992 universities and university colleges which prioritize widening participation and access to higher education. The original binary line has moderated itself with some pre-1992 universities being overtaken in the rankings by energetic rivals from the ranks of the post-1992s, but the shape of the system (and in the four nations of the UK) bears strongly the imprint of history and of a Mertonian process where the generation of reputational advantage, resource acquisition and research concentration have gone hand in hand. The adoption of similar research evaluation exercises in Germany, France and Italy, though consciously less extreme in their resourcing implications, serves to emphasize a growing trend in major European countries to reinforce research-based differentiation. Even within groupings of research-intensive universities, subsections of super-elite research universities begin to emerge.

Such distinctions do not apply in the smaller systems not least because the drivers for creating 'second-tier' categories of institution were geopolitical and economic (Portugal) or bred from concepts about regionalism and the rights of citizens (Norway). In these countries, and in Hungary elite universities exist, and are the most research-active, but their position is not a consequence of their research performance but much more of their inherent status based on their age, their place in the nation's history and their location in major cities. Thus in Hungary, Budapest is both the national capital and economically the most important city with a city school system which serves as a feeder to the nation's most famous university. A state scholarship system awarded on school performance (a model inherited from the Soviet dual entry system of state-funded and self-funded students) ensures that Eötvös Loránd University is able to capture the best qualified students from within Budapest with only a small proportion from ambitious students from outside the capital: ELTE takes 80 per cent of the students with the highest matriculation scores as compared with 5 per cent each at Szeged and Pecs Universities (24). Due to its influence with ministers, and because so many in government are its alumni, the university is able to protect itself to a much greater extent than other universities from state intervention. In Portugal, the Universities of Lisbon and Porto occupy a similar role to the Universities of Oslo, Bergen and Trondheim in Norway though these Norwegian universities fit much more into an existing Scandinavian community of research universities than into systems with such large reputational differentiations as can be found in Hungary and in other central or southern European systems. Moreover, in Norway the status divisions between the major institutions and the rest are much less than in Hungary and Portugal: although Oslo must be regarded as a university with a high international ranking, this is not reflected in public perceptions in Norway. As one senior academic explained:

> The way that students try to manoeuvre this market is… a reflection of a relatively low status difference between institutions so… students wander between universities and former colleges, now the new universities, so to speak,in a rather free flowing way. So it goes both ways. There are a lot of students who started at the University in Oslo but then migrate to other higher education institutions in Norway and vice versa. (25)

One might see the older 'elite' universities in Hungary and Portugal as flagship institutions as in the multiple state university systems in the United States, except that 'flagship' implies the leadership of a fleet of institutions. Eötvös Loránd, Lisbon and Porto Universities do not lead a fleet of universities, however, but stand as the envied apex of their higher education systems, drawing students away from provincial institutions to the much more expensive cities and looking inward towards government in their own self-interest rather than outward to the needs of their systems as a whole. This is not the position to be found in Wales or Scotland or in the more integrated system in Norway.

Diversity in European systems

The foregoing illustrates the diversity of higher education in Europe and within the different European systems themselves. This diversity stems from the historical processes which created the size of the systems and, particularly in respect to the 'second tier' of institutions, from geopolitical factors which vary sharply between one country and another. Three major factors seem to affect the system architecture. The first is simply the size of the system – it is possible to make reasonable comparisons between the UK (or England after 1992), Germany and France, but it is much less useful to compare any of these with Hungary, Norway or Portugal. In the UK, the expansion of student numbers over the period 1990–2020 was achieved by unifying the system and expanding the number of institutions, upgrading the polytechnics in a single legislative exercise and thereafter progressing the process of institutional upgrading incrementally as colleges grew and developed. But at the same time the resource implications of successive research evaluation exercises re-enforced the differentiation between the original university system and the rest. In Germany, expansion took place within a largely preordained university system and a binary line between the universities and the Fachhochschulen remained. In France, the rationalization of a fragmented system accompanied by widespread institutional mergers is now in progress with the aim of creating a unified sector covering both research-intensive and research-active universities. The implementation of research evaluation processes in Germany and France has been much less stringent than in the UK and in consequence the differentiation within their university systems has been less severe.

The second factor relates to how systems absorbed their 'second-tier' institutions into a unified sector. Regional considerations played little part in the upgrading of the polytechnics or Scottish Central Institutions in the UK (although they have been paramount in the more recent restructuring of the university system in Wales) but have great importance in Hungary, Portugal and, especially, Norway. But the steps governments have taken to produce unified systems, whether directed top down or bottom up, have accentuated the differences in the character of the university systems arising out of the regionalization policies themselves. In Norway, there is a strong public identification with the policies and an explicit sense in the institutions as well as in government of their contribution to the public good. In Portugal, while there is considerable idealism in the institutions as to their academic and economic mission, there is also a degree of insecurity in the gap in their resource base as compared to the older universities in Lisbon and Porto. In Norway, the discourse is more about democracy, the entitlement of people living outside the main conurbations and the importance of a shared citizenship, while in Portugal it is more about the problems of isolation in the country's hinterland, the direct economic benefit to their localities and the sense of needing to catch up with the rest of Europe. But the position is more uncertain in Hungary, where the political climate threatens institutional freedoms at a time when demographic decline and educational disadvantage raise questions about the resource base and the coherence of the system.

The third factor, the research dimension, again affects the large systems in different ways to the smaller systems. In the former, research evaluation processes are used to identify and reinforce research standing so that systems are restructured to compete internationally for reputation and resources. In the latter, a research divide between the long-established universities located in major centres of population and the regional institutions represents the natural consequence of the countries' history of higher education development, and while efforts are being made to incentivize research in these newer, provincially based universities, the evidence suggests that they are unlikely ever to be able compete with their metropolitan counterparts except in relatively specialized areas. The growing use of the title 'university of applied science' across Europe reflects the internal pressures for university status with the additional institutional privileges this may bring, but also serves to emphasize the differentiation between older classical universities and the provincial newcomers. (In Germany, the Fachhochschulen are permitted to use the title in English but not in German, a reflection of the extent to which reputation and image are critical components in an internationalized world of higher education.)

Much scholarly attention has been addressed to the concept that in Europe state steering has replaced direct state controls over higher education institutions. This study suggests that the position is more nuanced and variable. It is evident that the state is almost invariably interventionist in system management particularly in respect to research and that this can have a significant direct impact on institutional governance and management. The existence of research evaluation exercises and their outcomes in terms of reputations and resources can become dominant elements of institutional strategy and can determine resource allocation decision-making within academic communities. Questions of accountability, both financial and academic, may impose direct managerial interventions into university processes. (The establishment of the chancellor system in Hungary [see Chapter 3] provides a good example.) But there are variations in the extent to which states confine themselves to steering or mix steering and more direct involvement in institutional management. Whereas in Germany the federal government stands well back from concerns about individual institutions, it is clear that in some systems the links between heads of institutions and ministers on issues of individual institutional concern are close and may be productive for the institutions. In some systems (England, Norway, Portugal,

Hungary and Italy), the state has in effect devolved decision-making about bids for university status or the continuance of academic programmes to agencies specifically concerned with academic quality, distancing state involvement from critical decisions about system architecture. State steering thus comes in different shapes and sizes and its variations represent an important element in the diversity of European higher education.

3

The 'Modernization' of Institutional Governance

Any discussion of institutional governance within European universities must recognize at the outset the considerable diversity of forms of governance not just between national systems but within those systems, depending on individual types of universities and their different missions. In selecting the German, Hungarian, Norwegian, Portuguese and UK (England, Scotland and Wales as appropriate) for special study, an attempt was made to identify a cross-section of systems which would enable generalizations to be made with some confidence over European systems in general. Common activities such as the Bologna Process or the operation of the Horizon programmes seemed to point strongly in that direction but the evidence of our research findings suggests that caution needs to be exercised. Institutional structures remain heavily influenced by historical factors, by national political and legal frameworks and by institutional differentiations caused either by different histories or traditions or by different national perceptions of function. The most significant contrast between approaches exists between the forms of governance employed in the Anglophone universities and those in the rest of Europe, although arguably the reforms to give continental European rectors more managerial and strategic powers have reduced the differences. But it is also worth noting that institutional governance structures are subject to change under the pressures of massification, the demands of labour markets and restrictions on public expenditure in all European countries, so that a study of their different forms can represent something of an assessment of a moving target. The concluding section of the chapter attempts to summarize the main trends and the extent to which a common picture emerges.

Universities and the state – alternative patterns of development

The most significant division between the structure of university-state relations has not been between the Humboldtian and Napoleonic models but between the Anglophone model and the other two. Both the former envisaged a dominant managerial role for the state married to extensive academic autonomy within the institutions. The German structure owed much to the traditional role of the state acting as a protector of the institutions against church and other interference, with university-state relationships governed by law meticulously observed; in France, the state adopted a more centralized and directional role in respect to the institutions but, as in Germany, it was not interventionist in academic matters, leaving the academic community freedom to run its own affairs. In both countries, rectors and deans were elected posts from within institutions, ensuring that institutional leadership was firmly rooted in the academic community (Ruegg 2004). Universities were, in effect, part of the state and academics were privileged employees of the state, enjoying a high degree of academic but not financial and managerial autonomy; universities were funded to between 80 per cent to 90 per cent directly from state sources. The picture must, however, be qualified in respect to research where, in both models, the state through, for example, the Max Planck Society and the Frauhoffer Gesellschaft in Germany and the CRNS in France funded research in organizations separate from the university system. This did not mean that there were not distinguished research universities in both systems but that in particular the direction of scientific and technological research and the wherewithal to support it came from outside the universities themselves. Even today, as described above in Chapter 2, German universities are significantly benefited by external research funding through these bodies and independently through the Deutsche Forschungsgemeinschaft (the German Research Foundation (DFG)).

The historical picture of university-state relations in the UK was very different. From the date of their mediaeval foundations Oxford and Cambridge and the four Scottish 'Ancient' universities had been self-financing through fees, endowments and property ownership and existed as separate corporations entirely outside the state except that the state retained the legal authority to grant institutions the power to award degrees. In the later nineteenth century independent citizens in the major UK cities, following the example of London earlier that century, sought to generate funds to create a new generation of institutions intended to address the social, cultural and scientific and technological aspirations of their own communities (Vernon 2004). Having done so they went on to form the governing bodies of the institutions they had created primarily to see that they developed in the way they had intended and that the funding was appropriately spent, thus establishing the bicameral structure of an external lay-dominated council and an academic senate which has provided the pattern for the governance of UK universities to the present day. These institutions, which in the first decade of the twentieth century, having obtained charters and statutes from the state, became the first civic universities, were self-financing. Even when much later they became virtually fully funded by the state, and many more universities were established, the original structure with a lay-dominated governing body was retained. The adoption of a tuition-fee-based funding system in 2012 could be viewed almost as a reversion to their self-financing position before 1919 when the state first began to contribute regularly to their budgets, though it was very different in spirit and political intention; the appointment of the Office for Students as a Regulator was very much a twenty-first-century addition.

On the other hand, the continental European pattern, while creating a clear separation of powers between the financial and managerial controls necessary to run a university and the academic operations, located a substantial component of the necessary financial management in the states' own machinery of government to be exercised by the state, leaving the rector strictly aligned with the academic community and with only very modest managerial powers. On the Anglophone side the universities, as self-governing corporations, were fully independent of the state; the vice chancellor was both the academic and managerial leader of the institution but the institution was governed bicamerally by a primarily lay council, the membership of which included one-third academics nominated by the senate, which had executive managerial powers, and an academic senate/academic board which had what its legal instruments often described as 'supreme academic authority' in the institution.

But this distribution of powers was not immutable and became increasingly affected by a changing external environment. Over the period from the end of the Second World War, when the universities became fully funded by the state, UK senates accrued managerial powers at the expense of lay councils because their funding streams were essentially derived from formulae devised by the UGC which were more transparent to the academic than to the lay community. When massification began to take off in the 1980s, coupled with pressure on public expenditure, the state, through the Jarratt and the Dearing Reports (1985 and 1997), sought to reinvigorate lay governing bodies particularly in respect to their powers of financial control and to encourage them to assert their strategic role in the long-term direction of their institutions. In short, the balance of power between the senate/academic board and the governing body began to shift back to earlier times when lay governing bodies exercised real influence over academic development through their control of the purse strings. A definition of 'shared governance' in the Anglophone context was the extent to which the academic community retained a partnership with lay authority and the managerial powers of a vice chancellor (now described as 'chief executive' in many universities) in the operational and strategic decision-making (Shattock 2006).

In parallel, two sources of pressure affected the continental European model. The first was massification and the increasing inability of central governments to manage effectively the greatly enlarged higher education systems that expansion produced. A subsidiary but important consideration in periods of growing pressure on public expenditure was that the imposition of financial reductions became devolved, both for political and managerial reasons, to the institutional level. This strongly accorded with the principles of New Public Management which were widely adopted by governments across Europe leading to the assertion quoted in Chapter 1 that the task of the state was to steer rather than to manage the higher education system. A second pressure with the publication of international ranking tables was the realization of how far the performance of European universities had fallen behind that of American universities. The evidence, it was argued, pointed to governance ineffectiveness and particularly to the existence of lay governing bodies in US universities and the presence of managerial leadership of a kind impossible for rectors who owed their appointment to the election of their peers. (A contribution by Aghion *et al.* (2010) which stressed the importance of institutional competition based on academic performance was accorded a rather lower priority).

The effect of these pressures made a significant impact on institutional governance. If the state was to devolve its operational management of the system, it recognized that reforms were necessary at the institutional level: rectors had to become managerial leaders, not simply the voice of the academic community, and a lay element needed to be incorporated into institutional governance both to introduce greater financial accountability and to help shape institutional strategy. On the other hand, the state rarely attempted, at least by direct means, to reduce the historically entrenched position of the faculties which could exercise a powerful inhibition to governance change. In practice, in spite of frequent exhortations for 'modernization' from the EU Commission (CEC 2003, CEC 2005, CEC 2006), nation states did not respond consistently to calls for change to anything like a US or a UK model. Rather, what has emerged are modifications of pre-'modernization' governance structures which have built on areas over which either the state had greater control or which produced a lesser resistance from the academic community. The four countries whose patterns of university governance are described below are broadly representative of the patchwork of governance structures across continental Europe which have emerged from this process and are compared with the contrasting changes which have been taking place in the Anglophone systems.

Germany

In many ways the reforms to German university governance represent an exemplar of the changes introduced elsewhere. Germany has avoided many of the stress factors which affect Anglophone universities: its research evaluation system, the Exczellenz Strategy, is much less radical than the UK's REF; with Germany seeking 'distributed excellence' rather than an institutional hierarchy, universities receive about 80 per cent of their recurrent income from the state and do not charge tuition fees and, while there may be competition for research monies, the overall concept of a market in higher education is alien to the system. This affects the processes of institutional governance and reduces the incidence of top-down managerialism. Moreover, although the state has introduced legislation based in part to replicate US governance structures, German universities' positioning in the Clark triangle of coordination (Clark 1993) would still place them in the 'academic oligarchy' corner rather than in those of the 'state' or the 'market', an assessment seemingly confirmed by a decision of the Constitutional Court that all decision-making relating to teaching and research must be made by bodies where the professoriate have majorities.

This is not to say that the federal government has not legislated reforms in university governance encouraging Länder funding via a devolved block grant rather than through a predetermined allocation, requiring external (lay) involvement in the institutional board, enhancing the managerial and decision-making powers of the rector and removing the requirement that professorial appointments must be made by the relevant Land minister. But university staff remain public servants, and the role of the senate as the dominant decision-making body, the power of the faculties and the ability to elect, rather than appoint, rectors and deans is retained. Although there is considerable diversity in the way Länder have permitted university structures to be modified, the integrity of academic decision-making with Bavaria generally seen as being at the most conservative end of the spectrum and North Rhine-Westphalia at the other, the 'autonomization' of institutions has preserved an academic role in policymaking in a manner which contrasts strikingly with the position in the UK.

A university *Kanzler* (the chief administrative and legal officer under the rector) described the division of institutional governance provided in law in the following terms:

> [The rectorate is responsible for] the complete management of the university. Anything that is not regulated or is new falls within the remit of the rectorate. The senate is responsible – (and I would like to emphasise this) for [all governance decision-making covered by] regulations. The remit of the university council [or board] is to supervise the economic management of the rectorate. The chair of the university council is the supervisor of the rector and the chancellor.... It also adopts the university development plan. (1)

A strength of the German system is the relatively flexible character of the governance regulations. Thus although they specify that the university council must have external (lay) members, and that the maximum numbers of the council must be ten, they allow up to 50 per cent of the membership to be internal so that in this *kanzler*'s own university there are five external members (one of whom is the chair) and five internal. But cases exist where external members make up a majority or even the entire membership of the council. At this university, relations between the council and the senate were cemented by the chair of council being invited to attend senate meetings with the same facility being offered by council to the chair of the senate, but relations can be much less good in some other universities. External members are appointed by the Länder ministry but usually after taking account of a list of nominations submitted by the universities themselves.

The introduction of external members into university governance was controversial and met opposition in some universities, and evidence suggests that there is still some uncertainty as to the *raison d'être* of university councils. One external chair, who chose to list with pride the industrial and commercial background of his board which contained no internal members, was clear that:

> We see ourself as basically a strategic adviser… our key role is to initiate and support developing a strategy and to help getting acceptance [of it] inside and outside of the university. (2)

On the other hand, another external member was conscious that external members tended to be 'too far from the institution and not that much aware of the problems with the day-to-day business of an organisation like this' and noted that 'it's more common for the internal members… to be more involved in the day-to-day business of the university. So I would say that external members don't have the same sense of the organisation'. (3)

Another view, expressed by an administrator, was that:

> The internal members managed to bring up the real topics during the meetings of the university council and clearly said 'People, we are facing a problem here at the University' and they raised the awareness of the external members. (4)

The council's role in strategy may not be as decisive as intended, however: strategy development is formally a managerial task, and the responsibility of the rectorate, but before presenting a plan to the council, a rector will have to consult the deans and obtain senate support. Deans will themselves consult their faculty councils and will report on their views to the senate. As one senior administrator told us, 'I cannot see a strong strategy built solely by the rectorate in any university'. (5) It is not difficult to see how the rector's hands might be tied by the deans or the senate so that the strategy presented to the council reflects short-term academic priorities rather than a longer-term strategic vision.

In addition to strategy, the council also has an accountability role in respect to expenditure; it approves the appointment of auditors and the business plan. This translates into power over the budget. Again, the rector has responsibility for allocating the budget, but in practice the distribution to the faculties, especially if there is deviation between one year and the next, will be of keen interest to deans and faculty councils, to whom the distribution to departments is devolved, so that both the representative body of deans and the senate will become actively involved in whatever recommendations go to the council; a rector will have little or any influence over resources devoted within faculties to departmental academic priorities. Thus the actual, as distinct from the legal, authority of a rector can be severely constrained. This may particularly be the case in universities with medical schools where the ministry may allocate the medical school budget direct to the dean without reference to the rector or in research universities where as much as a third of a university's overall budget may be received from external research organizations, so-called 'third party' funding, over which a rector may have little control.

The most powerful body in the university is the senate, which elects its own chair and vice chair from within its members, and is dominated by a legally required professorial majority; the senate, in conjunction with the council, can dismiss the rector or the *Kanzler*; it also plays a critical role in a rector's appointment, although the legal decision must finally be made by a majority of the external members of the council. Everything regarding teaching and research must be discussed and resolved by the senate, which is supreme in all matters which are subject to external, that is, legislative, regulations. Internal regulations or guidelines issued by the rectorate can be discussed by the senate which can influence or reject them. As one senior member of a senate told us, 'the senate is the mirror of the different status groups of the university so when they [the rectorate] have a consensus, a consensus with the senate and also beforehand with the deans of the faculties', the senates should be regarded as the final decision-making body. (6) Critically, although the rector has the power, in most Länder, to make professorial appointments the senate may exercise a right to comment adversely on the qualifications or status of the name proposed so that a rector working to implement a faculty-recommended appointment may find it blocked by objections from other faculties.

Senates are very much driven by faculties. Deans in most universities are elected from within the faculties, though some universities have moved to appointing what are termed 'professional' deans drawn from other universities. Deans are budget holders for the faculties but are themselves subject to elected faculty councils which meet regularly. Deans are nevertheless powerful figures both in their faculties and in senate policymaking but must also be the mouthpiece of the views of their faculty councils. To that extent institutional policymaking may be significantly influenced, even dictated, by bottom-up opinion. Another comment, by a senior Land official, points in a rather different direction, namely that the reforms in German university governance which were aimed to give greater autonomy to universities and to provide a structure within which it could be exercised has, not made university management more effective but has been transformed into transferring that autonomy downwards so that deans and heads of departments have each been given reinforced authority to resist unwanted management from higher institutional levels. (7)

A further component of institutional governance is provided by the student body. It is clear from the major university in our study that a high level of student engagement is a critical element in institutional government. In this university, the students' union has four members on the senate, and, according to the deputy chair, they are 'very active, that is also very good' (8), and receive and comment on the curriculum vitae of candidates for professorial appointment on the same basis as academic members. Students are represented on faculty councils and departmental management committees. They are full members of senate committees and hold 50 per cent of the membership of the teaching committee, of which a student is also the chair. Students are not, however, just present to represent student interests but can play a wider political role within institutions. A professorial senate member described how close coordination in voting between academic members and student union members can occur over particular issues and how the students can play an overtly political role in pushing decision-making in particular directions:

> I think sometimes the university leadership… wants to satisfy the students more than they want to satisfy us and [when] the students are angry and go to protest, that is not good. They [the leadership] know us pretty well – professors don't really go to protest, they grumble a bit and we may be not so happy but then they go on doing their work anyway. (9)

A striking characteristic of German university governance is the dominant role still played by professors. In part, this reflects their traditional status reaching back to the Prussian university system. The sharp distinction between tenured professors and non-tenured other academic staff is partly a consequence of unreformed staff structures and partly the funding arrangements where the restrictions in long-term recurrent funding from the federal government are reinforced by the heavy short-term investment in research by the DFG and the major research agencies. In considering the powerful role in governance of the academic community (as compared, for example, in the UK) it must be remembered that this is exercised primarily by the position of the professoriate. The non-professorial academic staff, who comprise 75 per cent of the academic community, while they are represented at all levels of academic governance from the senate downwards, nevertheless comprise a minority in the academic decision-making bodies.

It is not difficult to identify areas of uncertainty, overlaps of authority and potential points of friction in German universities, but this would be to ignore the strong ties of academic culture which the system engenders. What universities look for is to find a balance between the rights and interests of the different elements of the governance model. For the *kanzler*, it would be the close working relationships between the council, the executive board or rectorate and the senate or, as spelt out by an external (lay) member, 'a balance, a negotiation of power interests among the senate, the university board [the rectorate] and, potentially, the university council… a balance between academic, social and economic interests'. The external member went on to quote examples of where such a balance might be upset: for instance, where 'the executive board is the only decision-maker which determines the work of academic staff thus compromising the freedom of research and teaching' or ceding too much control of finance to university teachers so as to risk insolvency. 'It is certainly not easy', he concluded, 'to find a reasonable balance but I also believe there are different ways to achieve it and universities should be the ones to determine these ways'. (10)

Our evidence suggests that this statement underlines the essence of the German university governance model and should be regarded as one of the strengths of the system as a whole. The state has not sought to be unduly prescriptive in its legal provisions but its provisions carry authority; the organizational culture encourages discussion and debate not confrontation, though confrontation clearly does take place in some institutions; and the different layers of constitutional representation are able to respond flexibly to issues as they arise. The system encourages stability even when funding is problematic. A major virtue is that it gives high priority to the academic voice in university governance albeit it is strongly weighted in crucial areas towards the professoriate. On the other hand, a criticism might be that its governance wheels grind slowly and even with the injection of third-party funding from research agencies the level of institutional competition and the built-in roadblocks to quick decision-making are not compatible with concentrating institution-based research excellence to compete with institutions in the United States or elsewhere. A rector or even a dean may have the formal powers to build an institutional or faculty centre of excellence but internally this must be negotiated through a network of interests and interest groups. The timetable will be punctuated by pre-meetings, briefings, consultations and compromises as support is assembled for critical investments in new initiatives or long-term reinforcements of success. In many ways, the operation of institutional governance mirrors Teichler's account of intergovernmental negotiations at state and federal levels in respect to system governance (Teichler 2018).

Norway

The underlying traditions of Norwegian higher education are Humboldtian, thus linking it with the German system, but the impact of the Quality Reform legislation in 2000–1 and its subsequent implementation has taken it into some quite different directions. While both countries have policies in respect to regions in each case prioritizing the importance of maintaining a 'level-playing field' of provision across the regional landscape, they do so from very different perspectives. In Norway, the decision to remove the binary line between its traditional 'state' comprehensive universities and the higher education college sector, and its encouragement of mergers among the latter to form new regional universities of applied science, is at variance with Germany's policy of maintaining a large research-oriented university sector but retaining the Fachhochschulen as a separate, and in student number terms, smaller sector. In Norway, the result has been the concentration of state policies in a single Ministry of Education and Research working closely with NOKUT, reinforced by hands-on meetings with university boards, annual visitations of institutions and close personal links with rectors. The relative intensity of the relations between NOKUT, the universities and the ministry, while operated in an apparently collegial and permissive manner, is unlike anything else we have found in European higher education systems. A further difference is that with the replacement of the collegium by a university board containing external (lay) members, the universities themselves opted to abolish their senates, a primary actor in German university governance.

From the beginning of the Quality Reform process, the state recognized the special position of the existing universities with Oslo, Bergen and Trondheim all having international research reputations and offered them a choice of retaining the elected rector as chair of the board but requiring the appointment of a director to be responsible for administrative matters or opting for an alternative model where an appointed rector was recruited by the board for a fixed term, renewable once, but where there was no requirement for a university director; in this case one of the external members would chair the board. Perhaps unsurprisingly the older classical universities chose the first version but the newer institutions, including all the universities of applied science, the latter. In both scenarios the legislation envisaged boards of eleven members, four external (lay) members, the rector and four internal members plus two student members. In universities where an appointed rector was not a member of the board, a further internal member was elected; but as one senior academic told us, it did not really matter whether the rector or an external member chaired the board 'because the Ministry is still a very important power factor and they govern the institutions regardless whether they have an external chairman or not'. (11) Although the external members are not in a majority they carry political clout because they are appointed by the ministry, drawing, but by no means exclusively, from lists of nominations submitted by individual universities. It is clear that these external members bring something different to discussions on strategy. One internal board member commented that in seminars on a new ten-year strategic plan while the deans were more concerned about how the plan would affect their faculty, the external members 'wanted a strategy that is more a sort of statement and a political statement'. (12) An external member, with a strong financial background, saw the board's role not as 'spending a lot of time discussing very detailed things with seemingly very limited impact' but

> What we try to do as a board is to understand what are the overall objectives from the owner of the university, the Parliament, and the way the government puts that forward [in] the way we prioritise, the way we spend our resources so it is mainly... a strategic oversight function. (13)

Another external member, a banker, told us:

> I'm not going to focus on one particular faculty or one particular department or one particular employer group. I'm going to think about what is good for the university as a whole, as an institution

and he went on,

> in the long run... how can this university maintain and improve its status nationally and internationally. (14)

These boards are not rubber stamps but conduct heavy business, meeting, for example, to scrutinize the quarterly accounts – one at least meets on average eight times a year, four each semester. How they operationalize their business depends significantly on whether they serve one of the original universities and are chaired by an elected rector or one of the newer institutions where the chair is an external member and where the rector is appointed by the board. In the latter case the fact that the internal members are in a majority helps to ensure that the appointment is 'not out of tune with the university' (15).

The board also appoints the deans though on the recommendation of the rector. The universities of applied science are much more unionized than the older institutions and the trade unions represent major interest groups in institutional decision-making, so much so that before agenda and papers are issued to the board, a rector may need to discuss the issues with the unions. However, as one rector argued, the structure is collegial: 'we have this Nordic model of negotiations when we make decisions and it works'. (16)

The absence of a senate has had two very important effects on the governance structure. In the first place it has moved decision-making up the governance chain: more seems to be decided at board level and universities have established executive committees chaired by the rector comprising pro- and vice-rectors, deans and the senior administrator (and in some universities vice-deans and student representatives as well) which carry out university business, initiate strategic planning and perform a central management role. More significantly the absence of a senate gives even more autonomy than in Germany to faculties in respect to academic business. Statements such as 'we don't accomplish much unless we have the faculties with us' by the member of an executive committee (17) or 'we do not overrule something that is coming from the faculties' by an external member of a board (18) attest to the privileged nature of the faculty in Norwegian university governance. Just as an elected rector cannot be dismissed by the board, so an elected dean cannot be dismissed by the rector, although this protection may not be as significant as it sounds as elected deans are increasingly being replaced by appointed deans.

In the Norwegian decentralized system, deans have delegated authority over their faculty budgets and are effectively immune from intervention by the rector or the board. Faculty budgets are based on disciplinary norms and student numbers and are funnelled direct to faculties, with only 15 per cent of funding left to be decided centrally, thus leaving the rector, the executive committee or the board with little power to prioritize or cut back on activities through resource allocation. One further consequence of the faculties' autonomy is that without the prescribed privileging of professorial power in decision-making apparent in Germany, the Norwegian academic has considerably more freedom in participating in faculty governance or in initiating new teaching or research programmes. Students, on the other hand, while represented on the board and in faculty councils, and by custom having regular meetings with university officers, are rather less influential without representation on an all-embracing policy body like a senate.

Comparing Norway's institutional governance structure with Germany's, one finds a much closer and more integrated linkage between the universities and the state than either at Länder or federal level in Germany. Lacking a senate, a central academic body to control or challenge the executive, Norwegian academics and students seem more distanced from participation in central institutional governance than is the case in Germany. On the other hand, the faculties have more autonomy and independence even than in Germany, with the deans acting as a sort of hinge between the academic community and management. When deans are appointed by the board, not elected, the balance between top-down and bottom-up governance can be tipped in the direction of top down but, as a senior academic argued, in a system like this much depends on the 'interplay between actors'. (19) We found little evidence of dissatisfaction in the academic community.

Hungary

In Hungary senior figures in the higher education emphasize its Humboldtian origins. Like other Central and East European countries, after the collapse of communism the Hungarian system reverted to the governance structures of the pre-communist era. Attachment to these structures as part of the mood to restore the pre-communist past inhibited the kind of system-wide reform that took place in Germany and in Norway and 'modernization' was only tackled piecemeal. Moreover in Budapest, Hungary possessed a dominant historic capital of cultural and intellectual, as well as political importance that it had inherited from the nineteenth and early twentieth centuries and which gave the University of Budapest, now Eötvös Loránd University (ELTE), a special status in national life; its internal governance structures served as a model for other pre–Second World War university foundations. Thus like Norway and Portugal, and unlike Germany, Hungary has, in effect, two tiers within its university sector except that in Hungary it has only one university in the top tier, the dominant ELTE, which recruits the top 10 per cent of the student age group, and its alumni make up a high proportion of the country's ministers and senior civil servants. Policymaking at both state and institutional levels, especially in the older universities, is tinged with a consciousness of the standing and historic institutional structures of the Austro-Hungarian Empire.

One senior non-academic critic condemned the effect of this mode of thinking on policymaking in the words: 'ELTE is world famous in Hungary'. (20)

Prior to the 2021 reforms the senate, to an even greater extent than in Germany, was 'the supreme decision-making body [of the university]… everywhere in Hungary' (21) and might have fifty to sixty members, 25 per cent of whom were students depending on the size of the university. It elected the rector, subject to final approval by the prime minister, and had the power to dismiss them; it approved professorial and associate professorial appointments, new teaching programmes and the university budget. External (lay) involvement in the governance of universities was correspondingly less than in Germany: the consistory, a body of three external and two internal members, was charged with accountability responsibilities, but although required to approve the university budget, it was required to submit it to the senate for final approval. The senate, however, represented to a great extent the voice of the faculties which contributed the majority of its academic representation. The faculties themselves were highly independent including in how they spent their budget allocations and, as a senior academic stated, even before the 2021 reforms 'in essence university management does not exist or to a very limited extent, that is to say formally it exists but has very little power… the university budget does not dare to interfere with the faculties'. (22) The faculties elected their own deans, had their own administrative staff and controlled their own expenditure, except that universities were so underfunded that faculty expenditure was almost entirely taken up in salary costs, leaving no room for new academic development. In these circumstances the senate became the arbiter between faculty budgetary demands. Reconciliation of a university budget might involve faculty councils, deans' councils, conciliation committees and eventually after many months of argument a vote in the senate where inevitably some faculties were aggrieved at the final decision. The senate's role was not, however, effective enough to prevent individual faculties from committing themselves to significant overexpenditure and, even for some faculties, to seek to mitigate this, by borrowing from faculties in surplus. In the senates' defence, universities were facing severe reductions in income: between 2008 and 2012 OECD reported that expenditure per student fell by 15 per cent at time when student numbers were falling by 7 per cent (OECD 2017). As a result each year the state was forced to roll deficits forward which were either endemic to the universities' economic situation or, where the rector or the director general of economics was unable to control individual faculty, overexpenditure.

The state's solution was draconian in the exercise of legislative power to invade university autonomy, unparalleled across modern Europe. Essentially it was to impose on every university a new non-academic senior officer with financial powers which overrode the powers of the rector, the senate and the faculties and who was answerable directly to the government and not to the university authorities. The title of the new post was 'chancellor' but should not be confused with a German *Kanzler* who, as the chief legal officer in a German university, is answerable to the rector and works within the constitutional structure of the institution not superimposed above it. At first sight the chancellor appointment might be seen simply as an arbitrary move to clean up an untidy financial situation across the university sector but in fact it appears to have been the cornerstone of a wider restructuring of the university system. Thus a minister claimed that while Hungarian public universities were 90 per cent financially dependent on the state, the University of California, Berkeley, also a public institution, was only 11 per cent dependent on the state; by analogy Hungarian universities should seek the same degree of assumed independence. Since the powers of the rector under university autonomy prevented state intervention, the post of chancellor was introduced to be responsible for the 'operational activities 'of a university in order to prepare it to achieve a greater degree of financial independence so that it could become entrepreneurial in attracting international students and applying for external funding for research. The minister took credit for the fact that the appointments had been successful and that the financial difficulties the sector had experienced had been largely eliminated.

But this was only the first step: 'the next bigger project is that we want to get universities out from the state structure and to let them operate as a normal university' (23) (no definition of a 'normal university' was given). The model for the reform was Corvinus University, previously the University of Economics, where 'they want to create a chartered university which is governed by a kind of association or foundation' (24) and where a chartered university could claim total autonomy in financial and strategic planning. The problem with the policy, however, was that taking Berkeley as an analogue did not take account of Berkeley's academic eminence or of the very different economic and research climate which existed in California. Moreover Corvinus, which in spite of its university title represented essentially a business school range of disciplines, offered a much more favourable prospect for a successful foundation-based institution than a multidisciplinary, multi-faculty university. The Corvinus model was, however, extended to all twenty-seven public higher education institutions in 2021; six universities declined the invitation. The invitation was 'sugared' with a handsome 'dowry' extended over several years but qualified by requirements to meet new student targets and to realign institutional strategy to national and regional priorities.

But before this, the imposition of the chancellor regime had created enormous strains within institutional governance structures. At the organizational level the chancellor took over the operational management of the university, including the functions of the secretary general and the Director General of the Economy, direct authority over all the administrative staff including the financial staff located in the faculties, leaving the rector responsible only for the office dealing with academic affairs and administratively the academic staff. One academic summarized the position:

> Before the chancellor's system came in everything belonged to the rector; when the chancellor came in, under the rector there remained one organisational unit, the Education Directorate – all the others went under the chancellor. The rector just became a formality. (25)

The chancellor was empowered to overrule the rector and the senate on all financial matters. Although before the imposition of the chancellor system the role of the rector was limited to little more than reconciling internal arguments rather than deciding on new academic initiatives, it is clear that, as one rector put it, 'the centre of power moved from the rector very much towards the chancellor because of the money'. (26) Another rector said:

> Basically on paper the rector is the *numero uno* of the university but actually in order to do anything which has significant fiscal consequences we have to have agreement from the chancellor and, since almost everything on the education and academic part has such responsibility or consequences, it is actually a very clumsy system. (27)

Individual universities learned to work with the system and some academics expressed gratitude for the improved financial stability which it has delivered but overall there was deep concern within the academic community over the infringement of university autonomy which had taken place. A key issue was the centralization of financial decision-making, with the academic community seeing the move as implying that a university should operate 'like a huge "multi company"'. (28) They opposed the internal restructuring of the administration into 'a unified operational model' (29) as severely weakening the power of academic decision-making particularly at faculty level. These pressures were intensified by national changes in budgetary arrangements which incorporated faculty-based student number targets and the decentralization of building maintenance costs, all of which moved 'the centre of power from the rector to the chancellor'. (30) As one senior academic commented, 'in this new structure the real power is with the chancellor and everyone knows it'. (31) A key element of academic criticism was the insertion of a non-academic into areas of academic decision-making. The strength of feeling can be judged by the decision of two faculties in one university where thirty posts needed to be lost to terminate the staff contracts themselves:

> We did it here within the faculty leadership precisely because we wanted to avoid the chancellor deciding on an *ad hoc* basis. We tried to resolve it with retiring colleagues who were already at the retirement age and on the basis of scientific criteria and performance criteria (senior academic). (32)

A feature of the chancellor regime was, and remains, their very close connection with government: their appointments were made outside the university and at ministerial level (and formally, like the rectors' appointments, were confirmed by the prime minister), and they meet in conference together monthly and submit detailed monthly reports on their institutions to the minister. There is a Chancellors' Club which provides an inner channel of communication with the state. Further to that with the introduction of the 2021 reforms the foundation boards have now become the main channel of communication with the minister replacing the Rectors' Conference.

The new reforms continue the process of subordinating institutional autonomy to state direction. The new boards comprise an external (lay) majority of members contracted for at least three days full time per week and in most universities remunerated at levels above that of professors. Each board contains active national and regional politicians, most often the university chancellor, a senior academic and may or may not include the rector. Its remit, put simply, is the management of the institution, its strategy and the production of its financial plan. In addition the legislation provides for a three-person external overseeing body and the appointment of a separate person responsible for auditing the accounts. The boards replaced the consistories, previously established in 2006 and based, according to a senior civil servant, on the boards of regents of US public universities. These, however, were five-person bodies with external majorities appointed by the minister which had been required to set the institutional budget subject to approval by the senate. This was no great loss: in one university where we interviewed the chair of the consistory confessed to never having met his fellow external members (33) and the leader of the students' union called it a 'façade body' (34) but gave some qualified support to the chancellor system on the grounds that 'in a lot of places it was needed'. (35) At another university a single meeting only was held to discuss the five-year strategic plan. (Because, in this university, the chair was a very senior external figure if there were particular issues over finance 'we either write a letter or I personally go and talk to the minister or whoever is in charge of that part of higher education' [36].) This was not a solution to the problems as then perceived in Hungary's universities.

It is not surprising – with student numbers falling in the system, high levels of student drop-out, funding levels apparently in decline, the autonomy of universities under threat and the authority of the rector undermined – that staff, even in the oldest and most prestigious university, feel a profound sense of insecurity: 'there is no perspective that you can see ahead in the long run'. (37) They are concerned for the long-term stability of the university. Hungary is paying the price for not embarking on a consistent modernization programme and for imposing reforms piecemeal without the support of, or contribution from, the academic community. It lays stress on its Humboldtian traditions but shows little inclination to draw lessons from its German neighbours and the way they have distanced themselves from direct political intervention. The Hungarian university system does not represent the modern European view of a system 'steered' by a government anxious to preserve institutional autonomy but rather as a system to be reformed by arbitrary actions to conform to a nationally conceived vision of a public sector of the economy characterized by excessive subservience to the state. As one academic told us, 'the current government doesn't like autonomy' and seeks to eradicate it whenever it can. (38)

Portugal

There are important common features in the contexts within which the Hungarian and Portuguese higher educations exist. Both countries have sought to engage in abrupt major reform in the turbulence following political regime change – Hungary from the fall of communism, Portugal from the end of the Salazar dictatorship; in each case the position of the universities was a key element in the movement for political reform. In both countries the systems have been seriously underfunded, in Portugal particularly in the period of the downturn of the economy post 2008, with the consequence that academic salaries are much lower than the average in many European countries and academic recruitment has been more or less frozen and promotions severely restricted; mobility between institutions has, in consequence, been negligible. However, the morale of the two systems is quite different: in Portugal academic staff continually refer positively to the democratization that has taken place within institutions, bear witness to 'the culture of freedom' that exists inside the university (39) and welcome the greater opportunity for academic participation in institutional governance provided by recent reform (40), while in Hungary academics are concerned about the uncertainty and apparent insecurity in their professional lives.

These differences stem from a number of factors but are certainly in part due to attitudes in government where in Portugal senior government figures applaud both the system's progress in research and the anchor roles played by the polytechnics/universities of applied sciences in their regions, whereas in Hungary the tone is much more of criticism: the inability of institutions to manage resources, the lack of entrepreneurialism, the failure to win a larger share of European research funding.

These differences have important impacts on institutional governance in Portugal and outweigh concerns about increasing bureaucracy in the system and the tradition of state control: 'regulating a lot of detail and controlling a lot of the detail which is still embedded in the system in some ways'. (41) The relationship between the council of university rectors and the government and the existence of a meeting twice a year between the rectors' and the polytechnics' councils and the government suggests the existence of a continuous dialogue and a working partnership between the state and higher education that does not exist on a system basis in Hungary.

Although the formal structures of institutional governance appear outwardly to be the same, the internal balance of authority and managerial decision-making between the two systems is sharply different. The most critical difference lies in the authority of the rector in Portugal, who may hold appointment for four years, renewable for only one period of four years. On appointment, rectors may recruit their own teams of vice-rectors and pro-rectors and heads of administration which 'decide on how to manage the issues of the university' (42) including the management of the budget. Unlike in Hungary, the academic council, the senate, is advisory only and does not have executive powers. It is a large representative body that meets to express opinions on proposals made by the rector, its own committees or the faculties on which the rector has authority to make the final decision. One rector described its role as being that of 'a parliament'; not all universities even have an academic council (43). By far the most important body, under the rector, for the governance and management of the university is the council of deans where the rector seeks to reconcile conflicting arguments from the faculties. In effect, Portuguese universities have cut out senates as decision-making bodies, leaving the rector to deal directly with the elected deans themselves seeking to advance the interests of their faculties. As in Hungary, the faculties are highly independent bodies with considerable financial autonomy and contain their own subsets of councils and academic departmental councils to which the deans are ultimately answerable. For instance, although they do not hold their staffing budgets, they are permitted to build up their own surpluses, which they can use to loan funds to faculties facing deficits. However, a senior professor, a member of a group advising the rector of one university on amendments to the formula governing faculty allocations in the light of fluctuations in student numbers, equipment and other costs, made it clear that while the rector could redistribute faculty budgets, his power did not extend to amending allocations within a faculty: 'we cannot go inside of what happens in the faculties because they are their own bodies'. (44) A rector's powers while extensive in questions of management and high-level strategy do not, therefore, extend to protecting or reshaping academic departments where the fundamental determinants of the academic performance of the university are vested.

At the highest level of governance, general councils in Portugal are integral to the functioning of the institution and occupy a position similar to governing boards in Germany or Norway. General councils not only select the rector but are required to approve the rector's plans, approve the budget for the year and approve a strategic plan but do not have executive power to impose their own vision over the rector's. Nevertheless, it is clear that institutions are strategic in the way they draw up lists of names to submit to the ministry for appointment to membership of general councils, seeking people who can actively contribute to making strategy at meetings in Brussels, or on the national scene; internal staff are positive about the resulting input to the institution. This is perhaps particularly felt in strategic planning where consultation throughout the institution would be the norm. Here the power of the rector to pull a plan together and reconcile the ambitions of the different faculties was a critical factor. As one senior administrator commented, 'it was impossible to have a strategic plan if the deans did not themselves believe in that plan of action; it was I would say crucial to the university'. (45) Now he claimed, 'I think they understand that we need to be together to be stronger to do well'. (46)

Unlike the former consistories in Hungary, whose operations were largely invisible to the academic community, general councils in the Portuguese system met regularly, around six times a year, and are an accepted part of the governance process. Most significantly, unlike Hungary, where the consistory's approval of a strategic plan was only part of a process which culminated in approval by the senate, the general council, as the senior body in the university, is itself the final point of decision. Some universities also have public foundation status, with the external members acting as trustees on behalf of the ministry to ensure that institutions are operating within the law and that assets are being used appropriately, but in practice this appears to make little difference to the operation of general councils or to the very real autonomy of the universities.

However, perhaps the greatest contrast with the Hungarian system is in regard to research. Whereas in Hungary, research seems to be valued less as the necessary academic function of a university and more as an important element in the diversification of the institutional income base, in Portugal, thanks to the active encouragement of the National Foundation for Science and Technology, universities have been encouraged to collaborate in quasi-independent research centres and institutes. These are jointly run by the participating institutions on sites mostly located away from the lead university's campus. From the research perspective this system has three great advantages: it provides research opportunities for staff in institutions which are not themselves particularly research active, it offers a supportive research entry point and research facilities to newly appointed staff and in some cases a remission of teaching load and it concentrates individual research strengths which might otherwise be dissipated around the university system. It also enables the foundation to have direct contact with the research enterprise rather than being only able to do so through a central university bureaucracy. As noted in Chapter 1, however, this latter advantage has had the effect of weakening rectorial authority and tends to drive a wedge between the research and teaching functions of the universities. Nevertheless, in the short run, it has provided a shot in the arm for research performance in the Portuguese system.

England, Scotland and Wales

All four nations follow the Anglophone structure of institutional governance described above with a council or governing body (or court in Scotland) as the corporate decision-maker chaired by an external (lay) member, a vice chancellor leading what is variously called an executive board, a senior management team or simply the vice chancellor's management group, a senate or academic board chaired by the vice chancellor, faculty boards and academic departments. These structures parallel what we find in Germany, Norway, Hungary and Portugal except for the absence of a senate in the Norwegian system, but the balance of authority and status in decision-making is very different. It should be added that in making comparisons the UK situation is complicated by the fact that polytechnics and colleges upgraded to university status from 1992 onwards have a more top-down managerial constitution than the pre-1992 universities: their governing bodies contain a lower academic representation, the vice chancellor is automatically acknowledged as the chief executive and their academic boards are restricted to narrowly drawn academic business and do not extend formally to institutional strategy which is reserved to the vice chancellor and the governing body. In the years since 1992, practice in pre-1992 and post-1992 institutions has become blurred: councils in pre-1992 universities, in reducing their membership to around twenty to twenty-four, have reduced their academic membership from a notional one-third to much lower figures, and academic boards in post-1992 universities are more likely to be consulted on strategic plans; both pre-1992 and post-1992 universities have entrusted policy and management to powerful executive committees led by the vice chancellor which may or may not have the deans in membership; most, if not all, vice chancellors see themselves as chief executives.

These refinements are by no means as important as the movement in the balance of power between these bodies, most notably in respect to the role of the governing body. Here the state has exerted continuous pressure to encourage lay governing bodies to exercise much greater formal control over institutional policymaking to the extent that in many universities they have begun to function more like company boards, cross-examining the executive on details of institutional performance and inserting themselves by right into policy issues. Shattock and Horvath describe this as the 'laicisation' of university governance (Shattock and Horvath 2019). There remains variation in the extent to which this 'business model' has currency, depending in part on the research intensity of the institution. (Oxford and Cambridge, for example, have resisted the encroachment of any form of external governance in the constitutions of their institutions.) But even in its weakest examples where governance is most obviously 'shared', the position of the governing body legally and in practice contrasts sharply with the institutional boards, general councils or the former consistories of Germany, Norway, Portugal and Hungary. (It is too soon to attempt any comparison between the new governing boards in Hungary with the powers exercised by governing bodies in the UK.) In the UK the chairs of governing bodies have their own consultative body, the Committee of University Chairs (CUC) covering England, Wales and Northern Ireland (and a similar body exists for Scotland), which publishes a Higher Education Code of Governance as a guide to the sector. The code contains forty-four paragraphs on the responsibilities of governing bodies in regard to accountability, sustainability, institutional reputation, inclusion and diversity, effectiveness and engagement which for the purposes of comparison can best be summarized in the following two paragraphs:

> The governing body is responsible for the mission, character and reputation of the institution and therefore sets its values and standards that underpin the institutional strategy and operation.
>
> The governing body must be engaged in development of the institution's strategy and formally approves or endorses the strategic plan in accordance with its constitution and the expectations of stakeholders including students and staff.
>
> (CUC 2020, paras 2.1 and 2.2)

Both provisions would extend lay governance a good deal further than would be acceptable to the academic community in most of continental Europe.

Twenty-five years ago, senates in the pre-1992 universities were the main policy-forming bodies, but now their roles have been diminished with the rise of the governing body and of the internal authority of the vice chancellor's executive body. With all the key academic positions, pro-vice chancellors, deans and heads of academic department as well as the vice-chancellors, being appointed rather than elected, the academic community finds itself managed by a core of academics most of whom could be described in the German scene as 'professionals' answerable to the vice chancellor not collegially to their academic colleagues. The traditional integration of the academic community with institutional policies, fostered by the election of senior academics to pro-vice-chancellor and dean roles and to headships of departments, which was never present in the post-1992 universities, is in severe decline. Senates, too, have lost authority and in many institutions have become more of a rubber stamp for policies advanced by the executive than bodies willing to challenge the executive (Shattock and Horvath 2019). It would be a mistake, however, to conclude that these changes have wholly altered the character of UK universities: Shattock and Horvath find that:

> It is evident that collegiality, freedom of discussion over academic matters and intellectual exchange about teaching and research continue to flourish 'below stairs' at faculty, school and departmental meetings but the picture

that emerges is that it does not penetrate the higher reaches of institutional governance.

(Shattock and Horvath 2019, pp. 122)

The Anglophone model of university governance has never lent itself to the level of faculty independence and devolved powers (except perhaps in medical schools) to be found in continental Europe. Top-down moves have been made to decentralize resource allocation or to merge departments to create schools of studies on grounds of efficiency or economy but it would be impossible to imagine in the Anglophone context the kinds of caveats that continental central university authorities enter in regard to overruling faculty views and demands. Faculty independence thus creates a vehicle for a direct academic intervention into institutional policymaking via the dean but also safeguards academic departments' interests from interference from the centre. It can also, however, have the effect of separating off the central decision-making authority from the wellsprings of academic performance and isolate academic staff from wider concerns within the institution. In the Anglophone world, academic interests are much more centred in the department than in the faculty. Counterintuitively this seems, even in the more neoliberal mode of governance now in operation, to open up dialogue and intellectual exchange across the institution at least as much as in the autonomous faculty model.

Funding mechanisms and institutional governance

Perhaps the greatest influence on institutional governance practice stems from the way institutions receive and allocate their resources. If there is a European tradition in funding policy, it is to finance institutions to something around 80 per cent of their budget through direct state grant. This was once true of the funding system in the UK, and it was only in the 1980s that the word 'market' entered the UK's funding policy vocabulary (Bird 1994, Shattock 2016). Direct funding from the state should offer institutional security but has attached to it the big risk that for whatever reason the state itself suffers a funding downturn as has been the case in Hungary and Portugal and that this is reflected in the grant. It, of course, also renders institutions more susceptible to redirection to reflect state-imposed performativity targets. However, where direct state funding is in place and stable, it facilitates university management structures which are themselves stable and lend themselves to a high degree of academic participation in governance because of the relative certainty of the funding stream. The more that marketization through student tuition fee and other mechanisms is introduced, the more management structures harden, decision-making moves upward in the institution and academic participation in governance is reduced as being indecisive when 'tough' decisions are required; the 'bottom line' also tends to replace academic priorities in criteria for institutional policymaking. These characterizations are clearly illustrated in this study with England, heavily subject to marketization, and with Hungary going down the foundation university route on the expectation of diversifying institutional budgets. To this extent England and Hungary represent one extreme of institutional governance and management, while Germany, Norway and Portugal offer more continuity in funding processes and greater certainty in outcomes, albeit in all three cases based on a measure of budgetary reduction.

Another important element within institutional governance is the impact of funding structures on faculties where, as in continental European universities, the dean or the faculty board is the budget holder and the rector is excluded from involvement in faculty allocation decisions. Direct state funding systems may assume or even indicate allocations to faculty areas, thus reinforcing faculty independence from rectorial priorities. The effect may be to undermine a state's attempts to strengthen central university governance and management and to build up resistance to change. It may also reduce academic innovation where the protection of existing interests squeezes out support for new initiatives. Marketization, on the other hand, tends to reinforce top-down control and strip authority from deans and faculty boards in the interest of central strategies for maximising income, ranking academic disciplines according to their ability to contribute to central budgets and emphasizing the value of restructuring to reduce financial risk.

In practice, all the universities studied were affected, to a greater or lesser extent, by markets. In countries where systems had expanded to respond to regional needs, such as Hungary, Norway and Portugal, the pressures of demographic downturn, the pull of institutions in historic cities and the decentralized nature of some campuses have all involved some loss of markets in a context where their student numbers are key factors in institutional funding allocations. In the UK, where, for historical reasons, almost all the most research-active universities are located in main cities, marketization has favoured the strongest institutions which have tended to expand at the expense of the rest (except in Scotland, where intake targets continue to be state controlled). This leaves a concern about the vulnerability of some universities which are notable for their part in widening access and which can legitimately claim to play an anchor role in their community.

One further element in the comparison between marketized and direct grant systems is the paradox that state intervention is more apparent where a market has itself been constructed by the state than in systems where funding is predominantly provided through direct state grants. The evidence seems to show that, in the former, governments have an itch to micro-manage marketized systems either to improve them or to bend them to emphasize new policy objectives instead, as one might have expected, standing back to see where the market leads. This increases the sense of uncertainty in these systems and reinforces the concentration of institutional decision-making in the hands of tightly drawn executive teams.

Institutional governance and system reform

The foregoing seeks to establish the diversity of institutional governance models within European university systems, as well as to illustrate their commonalities and divergences. What it shows is that, in all the countries studied, the role of the state *vis-à-vis* the institutions is expanding. There are variations between systems such as the high level of devolved institutional autonomy in Germany and the interventionist approach in Hungary, but in general the picture is of a growing erosion of the independence of institutional policy in favour of system management. In this context, perhaps the greatest example of convergence is the abandonment in England (but not in Scotland or Wales) of the intermediary body (the UGC and HEFCE) standing between government and the institutions. The Office for Students is not a successor body but has been established as a regulator, and as a regulator for teaching only, with research the responsibility of a separate body, Research England, answerable to a separate government department. Thus the UK universities find themselves for over 80 per cent of their activities, like their colleagues in continental Europe, operating in a climate where the state has a potentially direct relationship with the system, and are therefore more open to political intervention than when 'buffered' through some intermediary mechanism. The decisions first to impose the chancellor system and then the foundation idea on Hungarian universities represent extreme examples of this, but the pressure to extend the powers of governing bodies in England, while actually achieved with the connivance of HEFCE in its last days before dissolution, reflects the kind of reaction within government when trust has broken down between the state and university authorities. Indeed the establishment of the Office for Students itself, as the regulator of a government-created higher education market, bears the hallmark of an ideologically driven mechanism, the product of a directly political intervention in the management of the university system.

Against this, all the systems, with the exception of Germany, had the common characteristic of having a widely divergent set of institutions. Each also had a subset of historically highly prestigious universities which have tended to differentiate themselves from the rest and, because of their status, have been more able to resist or at least moderate the effects of state intervention. Universities in this category might include Oslo, Bergen and Trondheim in Norway; Lisbon and Porto in Portugal; ELTE in Hungary; Oxford and Cambridge, Imperial, Kings and University Colleges and the London School of Economics in England; Edinburgh and Glasgow in Scotland; and Cardiff in Wales. Oxford and Cambridge, for example, have shown no inclination to introduce an external (lay) element into their governance and the state has given up trying to persuade them to do so. A consequence is that the pressures for governance reform that might be imposed by the state are differentiated in their effects, falling most heavily on newer, rural or less research-active institutions and least heavily on institutions whose research standing and public reputation provide some measure of protection. Germany's 'distributed excellence' research system offers an important exception to this picture. Partly this is due to its constitutionally protected federal structure. Germany does, of course, have historically prestigious universities, but the policy of homogeneity between Länder and a dominant grouping of elite research universities has reduced the kind of in-system status achieved by some universities in the other countries studied and seems unlikely to emerge even with the encouragement of the Excellenz Strategy. The German system emphasizes institutional equality rather than the hierarchies that have arisen elsewhere; the consequences of this for staff and student recruitment, the prosecution of research and the international competitiveness of the system as well as for the autonomy of the system *vis-à-vis* the state are far reaching.

A significant issue in any review of institutional governance is to ask which elements are likely to encourage or inhibit innovation and creativity and drive performance. The evidence from this study, particularly from interviews with academics, confirms the view expressed in *The Governance of British Higher Education* (Shattock and Horvath 2019) that open structures encourage academic innovation and creativity and that 'a too dominant structure inhibits it, imposes restrictions on new thinking or creates decision-making hierarchies that are defensive in outlook, unreceptive to change and unwilling to take what might appear to be academic (or related financial) risks' (Shattock and Horvath 2019, p. 103). Two examples of the latter immediately spring to mind: the imposition of the chancellor system on Hungarian universities and the pressure to extend the role of external (lay) governance in English universities. On the other hand, the move in both Germany and Portugal to give greater authority to rectors seems calculated to provide universities with a more effective decision-making process as has historically been the case in the English, Scottish and Welsh systems. The evidence of a decline in the position of the academic council in Portugal and of the senate in the UK nations and the absence of a senate altogether in Norway raises issues that must be balanced against the primary governance role played by the senate in German universities, and against what appears to have been an overdominant role in Hungary before the 2021 reforms.

One of the key elements of the modernization of university governance and management has been the extension of the rector's powers into an executive body made up of senior university officers. This has improved coordination and institutional management especially as institutions have themselves grown larger and more complex. However, such bodies, particularly when designated as 'the senior management team', can all too easily become too authoritarian and detached from the constraints of academic opinion. The existence of a senate provides an important check on the expression of bureaucratic power and opens the door to bottom-up ideas which might not otherwise get considered at a university level if the only check on central authority is provided by, for example, a committee of deans. The great strength of the kind of faculty structures to be found in continental Europe is the protection they offer to the academic community against external intervention in the academic life of institutions. On the other hand, faculties can operate their own hierarchies and power structures which can inhibit openness to change and encourage conservative attitudes to innovation and creativity. Their role is primarily defensive. A senate, not dominated by faculty interests, is in a position both to keep a check on the executive and to serve as an academic voice on wider matters of university policy.

It is a truism that universities suffer intellectually as well as in other ways if they become disengaged from the societies in which they exist. This is one of the prime reasons for seeking the involvement of external (lay) members in university governance: the existence of governing bodies with a majority external membership has, until recent pressures, been one of the successes of the UK nations' approach to governance. Of the four continental European countries in the study, the German model is closest to the UK's because it permits institutional variations from a majority to 50:50 lay internal membership. In Norway and Portugal the ratio of lay to internal membership is much smaller, while in Hungary, on the other hand, the position is reversed. The lay members from Germany, Norway and Portugal from whom we took evidence indicated how seriously they took their role, particularly in regard to strategy. The lay chair of a consistory in a Hungarian university, abolished as a result of the 2021 reforms, went so far as to comment on the university he served on, however: 'I feel it is such a closed world'(47). In general external (lay) members represent an underused resource in continental European universities while being given too great authority in some but not all UK institutions.

If we were looking for significant convergence, it would be for long-run trends rather than decisive change. It is evident that there are moves in all countries except Hungary to give more authority to central decision-making within universities whether in the hands of a rector or vice chancellor or some sort of rector-led executive board, but moves to replicate the role of boards of regents in US public universities are a long way off in continental universities. The academic sensitivity to conceding more than a titular governance and management role to governing boards with external (lay) members in majority remains acute except in Hungary where the overseeing boards that have been imposed on those universities becoming foundations seem more like a sign of increasing central political control than a way of involving society more closely in university governance. Across the board the state is becoming more interventionist, less in Germany than elsewhere, and institutional governance is becoming more rather than less subordinate to state decision-making. The model of the state steering autonomous institutions no longer describes what one finds on the ground. And the abolition of an intermediary body standing between the institutions and the state, once the guarantee of the exceptionalism of the operational freedom and autonomy of the universities in England, offers the possibility of opening the door to a much greater convergence of the Anglophone system to a continental model where state direction within a framework of relatively limited operational freedom becomes universal except perhaps in the case of some research-intensive universities where success in research and national and international reputation may represent an enduring protection from the state's advance.

4

The Changing Participation of Students and Staff in the Governance of European Universities

There have been considerable changes in the main components of institutional governance across higher education institutions in Europe, often changing the balance of participation within institutions. While previous chapters extensively discuss the ways university executives and the state shape institutional governance processes, this chapter describes the participation of students and staff in their institutions' governance and explores how much weight students and staff carry in decision-making processes. Our findings show that the balance of representation of the components of institutional governance has made for important differences in how decision-making takes place.

Thus, while in the UK the involvement in decision-making of the academic community has weakened and given way to a much greater authority vested in the senior executive and in externally recruited deans, the autonomy of faculties in continental Europe and their ability to elect their own officers has been largely retained, leaving rectors and their senior executive teams with much less freedom of academic decision-making than in the UK. On the other hand, the student body has a much more prominent role in governance in continental universities than in the UK, with greater voting powers on senates and a more generalized political role in the affairs of a university.

In this chapter, while we cannot do full justice to the multiplicity of views and experiences shared by our interviewees, we aim to give an extensive voice to students and academics, to reflect their own views of their role and powers within governance.

Students in university governance

Across Europe, governments and universities argue that the student voice has increased in importance, and that student representation across university governance structures and bodies is much stronger than it has previously been. However, scholars of student participation in governance argue that, even from a formal point of view, this is not the case (Nielsen 2015, Brooks 2015, 2021, Klemenčič 2012). Our data supported such conclusions, as most student organizations we interviewed frequently argued that their formal inclusion in structures did not equate to increased influence. Also, as many of our interviewees stated, consultation and integration often meant co-optation as well: 'The government has felt that if they maintain a [good working] relationship with the student unions then it's less likely that we would be in the streets causing trouble', argued one UK student representative. (1) Radical politics existed despite student integration in governance, rather than because of it. At best, this only allowed for incremental change or no impactful change at all.

In addition, the issues student organizations prioritized were often influenced and steered by national political agendas and broader economic processes (e.g. housing, employment, mental health and wellbeing). That is to say that a complex set of difficult and important issues that were not prioritized for resolution on national political agendas fell to students and universities to deal with. To varying degrees, this created unwarranted stress, which became evident in recent years through an increase in mental health issues among students across continental European and UK universities.

A majority of the student organization representatives argued that overall, and increasingly, students experienced high levels of stress and felt less empowered by higher education institutions and national structures. We were surprised to discover that – from the students' point of view – having adequate funding for higher education institutions and student welfare organizations, as was the case in Norway for example, did not necessarily result in happier students or students who graduated in higher proportions. Other societal factors were also at play in defining what students could do. As will be seen in the following sections, while student advocacy and mobilization can make some important contributions to institutional governance, many of the issues that would need broad social consensus and system-level support could not be changed through student participation alone, or at least not quickly or significantly.

Student influence at national and regional levels

In each of the countries where we conducted research, the names of student organizations reflected different organizational structures:

> Norway: In universities, student organizations were called the Student Parliament. In each university – by law – it was required that there was also a Student Welfare Organization governed by students and working closely with the university's senior executive group and the student parliament. The National Union of Students in Norway became the umbrella organization under which each university's parliament fell.
>
> UK: In universities, student organizations were called Student Unions, and at national level the National Union of Students.
>
> Hungary: In universities, student organizations were called Student Councils. All were under the umbrella of the National Union of Students in Hungary.
>
> Portugal: In some universities there were Student Unions, and in some other universities there were Student Associations. At national level there was a student body called Academic Federation for Information and External Representation. In addition, in some regions where there were high numbers of university students, there were also regional representative bodies, such as the Porto Academic Federation and the Lisbon Academic Federation.
>
> Germany: In universities, there were Student Associations. The national-level organization took the name of the Free Association of Student Bodies.

Terms such as 'parliament', 'welfare organization', 'union', 'association', 'council' and 'federation' indicated the varied organizational forms student bodies took in different countries. These different forms had been determined by national legislative frameworks, but were also shaped by local institutional traditions, regulations, and practices. Therefore, even within the same country, the organizational practices of one student body might differ greatly from another similarly called student body from a different university. For example, one of our student representative interviewees from a Norwegian regional university argued:

> [Norway] Our university merged in the late 2010s, and… you had several student unions from several colleges, which came into one university. And no-one could agree on a structure, so they just took one from an established university… which is based on one campus, one city, one structure. And it doesn't work here. So, from 2015 to 2017 the student parliament was not functional. There was a lot of tension… So, what we did [when I came into office] was that we took one year to look at the organization, we found new structures, and we got them approved by the student parliament… There was no-one we could borrow any ideas from, but we are part of a national student organization. I have contacts with all the other universities, and when we made the change, the other universities came to us and asked, 'what are you doing, how is it working, can we have your regulations, your laws, can we see your new structure?' So now there are three other universities that I know of in Norway that are considering changing to our structure. (2)

However, one could also argue that – to some degree – the organizational forms that a student union was allowed to take within a country also reflected the – broadly understood – political role higher education student organizations were able (and were expected) to play within institutions and nationally. For example, the student parliaments of Norway and Germany ran their elections along political party lines that replicated to some degree those of the major parties of the country.

> [Germany] My role is representing 43,000 students. Which is difficult. In the student parliament we talk about different things which come up in the academic senate as well. Sometimes I already know what the senate thinks about a certain issue, and I can say that the students think that it is not OK to do this. But most of the time I don't really have the time to ask a lot of students what they think about this issue. That's why, like every other normal party, we make our points of view public when the election starts. We have one week where we can promote ourselves and then I really trust the students that they just vote for me because they are OK with my points of view. I'm a part of the Greens, so I think most of the students somehow

> know what I would stand for, and I try to act that way… The other three [student] members of the senate are not in my party; they have different views. That's normal. That's OK. But if there is a decision made in the student parliament, they also rely on that statement. (3)

In Norway, student parliaments understood their engagement with academic matters as having to be very broad and student representatives did not shy away from articulating these roles as political. Many student representatives were elected to the student parliament from lists that they called political party lists, mirroring the ideologies of different mainstream political parties.

> [Norway] We have different lists that are sort of political parties. I am, for example, from what's called the Labour List, and that is connected to the Norwegian Labour Party. But they don't all have to be political, we also have lists that are connected to the faculty, or lists [for students who] just want to party, so you can create your own list very simply. (4)

In contrast, in Portugal, student leaders often felt that if they were part of a university's student association and not an organization that was independent from the university, they could not address the broader issues at stake for students, and their roles were limited to participating in teaching and examination committees with their contributions being restricted to dialogues about study issues. As a student representative of one of the regional student federations explained:

> [Portugal] [We are not based in any university and so we only have minimal support from universities.] We have a very complicated [organizational] structure, but we want to maintain it because that way we have total independence to make our policies, and do not owe anything to anyone, so we can say whatever we want. (5)

Nevertheless, despite these differences in organizational forms, our interviews also indicated that – in essence – all student representatives understood their key missions to be the representation and protection of student interests within their organization and – if and when needed – also at regional and national levels. Our data also clearly indicated that despite attempts to de-politicize student movements – often even by the student membership of these organizations – many student organizations still saw their role as somewhat political and tried to engage with and connect to local-, regional- and national-level politics on matters that impacted on student life, including housing, fees, living expenses, student employability, environmental matters, sustainability and so on. As a student representative in a regional German university explained:

> [Germany] I would love to say [that we are representing our students] culturally and politically, but it's hard to really know what the students want, because most often the loudest voices are not the most important ones. But we have some critics who come, they are always the same people, but they are really consistent, who think that we are too Leftist, that [we shouldn't do] our events about feminism, or criticizing study fees for international students… and that we should invest our money in a different way. (6)

Similarly, a UK student union representative argued:

> [UK] In our elections people vote on 'I like that person's name. I like that person's photo. They are my friend, or my friends told me to vote for that person'. So, in terms of that, we are not very political. We don't have any political societies; however, we've had two set up this year. So, we've had a Labour Student's Society and a Socialist Worker Society established… When the Teaching Excellence Framework came out, we, as a student union, were like 'we are going to write a response to the Green Paper. Let's get involved. This is how it could affect you'. And there was no interest from the student body. It's not that they are not interested; I presume there are students who follow politics outside of university but just don't want to engage with it through the student union. Because we are not known to be a political student union anyway. (7)

In several countries, such politicization was much more changeable and opportunistic. For example, in Hungary, political parties, on occasion, used local student unions to influence university politics. On the other hand, the Hungarian national student union had, on occasion, been able to influence national politics, and was still regularly consulted on higher education matters by ministers and state secretaries. As a student representative in a large Hungarian research university argued:

> [Hungary] A Minister will not talk to a faculty president, but he will talk to the president of the National Committee of Student Unions (NCSU).

And these things are mostly going to the national level, but individual universities' student unions are the ones who delegate the members. We elect the president. We vote on these issues… Recently we started an Association of Humanities' Students. I was a founding member. It is a professional association within the NCSU. All the faculties of humanities are in it, and the Secretary of State is a constant guest at our meetings. And the teacher training strategy, the Humanities' strategy are all being created now with the help of this association and our recommendations were mostly included. (8)

In other countries, national networking and mobilization was relatively weak and ad-hoc, and had been weakened in recent years by different national policies and trends. For example, in England, the Office for Student's remit partly collided with the remit of the National Union of Students (NUS). This, and the fact that the NUS had run into serious funding difficulties over the previous few years, led to NUS losing significant powers and functions. The National Student Survey (NSS) in the UK gave an additional outreach and some lobbying power to student organizations. However, it was widely debated how much meaningful change students were able to achieve using the NSS as a leverage. It was well known that the most pressing issue for students in the UK was the burden of tuition fees and the lack of support for living expenses: on this issue neither local nor national student unions were able to achieve any meaningful changes, despite initial widespread student mobilization. As a UK national-level student leader argued:

[UK] Whilst there are ties with different organizations in the UK, and indeed with political parties, it's not been so clearly defined. And clearly, there are also quite big political tensions within the student movement that mean that it's more difficult to unite… There are also legal restrictions. They come mainly as a result of student unions being charities, and the fact that charity law means that they can't be as political as other organizations. And we saw in the 2015 general election, with the Lobbying Act, that that really stifled the power of the student movement, because it wasn't able to unite and pool funds to be able to challenge and lobby particular political parties. Although I think all the political parties made particular changes to their manifestos as a result of student lobbying, it didn't have the same desired effect as it could have had… But we are seeing a movement in the UK towards more direct forms of action in the student movement, as a result of, I guess, some of the legal issues and not being able to lobby effectively through what you would deem sort of normal, legitimate challenge. (9)

All national student unions, including those in the UK, networked with and maintained a membership in the European Student Union (ESU). However, as the UK NUS representative argued, while discussing matters across countries was inspiring, student unions were mostly left to their own devices to influence and change national higher education policy.

> [UK] I think [the global/international student movement] has a benefit more in terms of what the student movement can do for wider political issues. For instance, if we are dealing with problems that are global, so dealing with things like climate change, dealing with things like open borders, and immigration, these are problems which the student movement can unite [behind] and deal with. [However,] because of the kind of specificities of the educational issues in each country I think it's more difficult for an internationalized student movement to have effects in each state on their education systems. So, I see there being, through the European Students Union, much more of an impact on things that are international problems. (10)

Connections to and impact on national politics, including direct access to ministers and other members of government, varied greatly across countries. In Hungary, such direct relations were very person-dependent: if a local student organization was able to establish and negotiate a personal relationship with one of the ministers or state secretaries, they were able to maintain a frequent working and lobbying relationship. Local organizations that did not have that kind of personal contacts could still make their voices heard through the national union, but that took significantly more time and was much less impactful. In Norway even local student organizations had regular and direct access to the ministry, so they didn't need to go through their national student union. In Germany, practice differed from Land to Land, and most federal-level engagement was done through the national student organization, the Free Association of Student Bodies. In other countries, such as the UK – particularly so in England – local student organizations almost never saw a minister or a prime minister, and it was never the case that government members consulted directly with local student organizations.

In all our case study countries, students felt that there were regional- and national-level forces that had a great impact and influence on student life, and those forces reached beyond and above the powers of university governing bodies.

[Portugal] [At city level] we depend a lot... on our relationship with the people that are in power and try to influence some [of their] decisions. Because we feel if they don't want to hear us, or they do not agree with us, we don't have many [opportunities] to [voice our] opposition and try to make our case heard... If we [scale up] this discussion to the national level, it's even worse, we [have no forum]... to participate, so we depend a lot on the willingness of the minister to hear us out. This one does not have [the willingness]. It's very difficult to reach this minister. And very difficult to influence their agenda. (11)

[UK] I don't think higher education will prosper under the current government. I don't think the motives of the current higher education minister are in the interest of students. A lot of it is just about business, making money, getting students in the door but not supporting them, and that really concerns me... Higher education is just so turbulent at the moment and if we are being governed by the OFS [Office for Students] where we had to fight tooth and nail for a student representative to be on it, then I do worry about the future of higher education and how students will be represented in governance. (12)

In Germany, student officers expressed concerns that regional politics enabled interference with their activities, as the Länder could change regulations and make full-time attendance in all university courses mandatory, which would make it difficult if not impossible to conduct their administrative duties.

[Germany] It's really good that we have this chance to participate so much inside the university... we appreciate our possibilities and that's why we right now are concerned about the new ideas of the regional government... they want to minimize our power somehow, [because] it's a form of power that we are so visible... it's not unusual that the local press talks about students at our university because we are so engaged... Yeah, that's why [the regional government] tries to minimize our power. (13)

Student influence on institutional policy

Our findings showed that students in all our case study countries had a formalized role and frequent opportunities for input on various university bodies – from departmental education committees to faculty councils, academic senates and university governing bodies. In all twenty universities where we interviewed, the representatives of student organizations argued that students were listened to and their opinions mattered. However, many also argued that their opinion often counted only on the issues that were of importance to university leadership. Representation was less successful on the issues that were put on the agenda and mattered most to students. At one extreme was the UK, where most student union representatives felt that their consultation and representation rarely resulted in transformative or radical change that served students' interests. In Norway, on the other hand, student leaders argued that even if incentives for broader transformative change did not come from their ranks, they were able to represent students' interests successfully in such debates on governing bodies.

> [UK] [University governance] doesn't feel like it's driven by what's best for the students,... it's definitely moved away from being for students and it's more trying to just keep up in a competitive market, providing an education. But truly are students being consulted on what they would like from education, or what they would like to see in their education? I wouldn't say so. (14)

> [Norway] We are definitely not the people that... initiate the big ideas for [addressing] problems at our university, but I would say we are included pretty early on, to the point that we can sort of shift it in students' favour. And we are welcomed into most discussions, I would say. (15)

The fact that overall student participation in student organizations was low and had been steadily declining over the years, and that there had been occasional divisions within student unions, all contributed to weakening the student voice within institutions.

> [Hungary] It is difficult to move students towards public life, so they are not necessarily active, and it is becoming more and more noticeable year by year. In recent years, we have recognized as a student union that... we can only be effective if the students are unified... if we cannot move in the same direction among ourselves the leadership of the university won't take us seriously. This divide and rule strategy works well for university leadership, but not for us. (16)

Many student organizations also felt that they were somewhat unsuccessful in mobilizing students around broader social and political issues; if participation happened at all in such movements, it took place outside the context of the student unions.

> [Norway] [Students are not very active in the student parliament.] Participation is visibly declining... It is hard for students to know who we are. And what we do. And if it matters... This is a very large institution, and it takes time to move a mountain, so if you vote for something this year, then it might not happen within six years, and then you will not be here anymore. So, it takes time to see the results of what we do. (17)

> [Hungary] Since 2006, when this Bologna system was introduced... the time that students spend at university has been significantly reduced. That's why we are trying harder to reach people... They spend so little time here, and they also have to work, in addition to studying. I think the priorities have changed a bit at university: it's no longer about the experience. It's not about the community anymore. It's just about getting a degree and then a job. (18)

Our findings also indicated that, in many cases, the formal governance structures of student representation within institutions and in national legislation did not offer sufficient protection from senior academic leaders sidelining, dismissing or delaying student matters. As a result, the personalities of student presidents, their ability to network and build support in committees, academic senates and on boards, as well as the skills of their leadership teams greatly influenced the tone and efficiency of their relationships and success in their encounters with the executive. This also meant that in many of our case study universities, there was an unevenness in successful representation from one student administration to the next.

> [UK] I think it happens across the sector, where a lot of decisions are made outside meetings, so you have to do your networking first and find out who is on your side before you go into the meeting... So I've made it a priority to network... from my year as [a student union] vice-president, I was involved in the academic board, and... I saw it happening where people would be meeting and you'd see them sit on the sofa outside the room talking and then [they] would go in and support each other, so I thought OK. It sort of happened a bit with the previous [student union] president, but not so much. So, I made it a priority to build up a really strong rapport with the university staff this year; I have regular one to ones with all the vice-chancellor's offices... I'll look at what's coming up in committees on papers

and get their feel for things as well. With the board of governors, we always have a board dinner [the night] before the board; we meet, we have dinner, we have a bit of discussion, and even there I've built up a strong rapport with people. (19)

[Norway] We have monthly meetings with the pro-rector. And we also meet the rector and other people from the administration on a regular basis, in informal meetings,... dinners. And then we make sure to talk about things that are important to us. (20)

The fact that most student organizations had direct access to and good working relationship with the leadership team of their university did not necessarily mean that students felt empowered by such consultative meetings. It was often pointed out by student leaders that university executives used such occasions to co-opt the students' voices and legitimize their own decision-making.

[UK] The university's put too much [emphasis] on making sure that sabbatical officers are on committees rather than reviewing [whether or not] we really need a sabbatical officer there. Because it almost turns into a box-ticking exercise of 'oh yes, we have our student representative', even though... the majority of stuff [discussed on such committees]... doesn't really have an impact on our students. (21)

[Portugal] [In many university bodies students have 25% or more representatives but] the only way we can have leverage is if the professors do not agree [among themselves] with the position that they are presented with, [then] you have a chance of passing that through... (22)

In some countries, such as Portugal, Hungary and Norway, there were dual paths into senates and councils/boards: some student representatives were elected directly by the whole student population, while the student organization also placed student delegates on these bodies. This meant, on occasion, that the student voice was divided, but more often – if they were able to align their interests – the result was that students had more powerful representation.

[Hungary] The truth is that [it] is worthwhile for a rector or a dean to be in a good relationship with [the student union]. If there is a dispute in which the professors are not united, rectors can ask the student union's help. With our 25% presence [on senates], and with one-third at faculty level, we can successfully vote into power any pending decisions. This is a force that a university leader can use, if he then does whatever he can to make our lives easier. And that often happens. (23)

However, the extent to which students' voices had an impact in influencing policy change on university bodies varied greatly across countries: when they had a large number of student representatives on these bodies, and they were unified in presenting their position(s), their voice could make or break the outcomes on many important issues, including the election of a rector. This was the case in Hungary, Portugal and in Germany, where they have been able to tip the balance in many important votes. However, in Norway and the UK students had much less of a direct impact on outcomes. In these countries, student representation on university boards was low, and they were encouraged to see themselves as individuals who consider the interests of the whole institution. In these cases, the best way for them to achieve something was by lobbying and informally mobilizing other council members.

In addition, students were often presented with the dilemma of competing interests: representing a well-defined constituency (the student body) but being told by boards that they must step out of that role and vote based on the interests of the whole institution.

[Norway] I, and the other [student] board member, are not bound by the politics that the student parliament had taken, because by law we must see the totality of all the decisions; we have to take into consideration more than just the student perspective… That's one of the challenges maybe, being part of the [student parliament's] executive committee, and also the board. (24)

Finally, in some of the more decentralized institutions, where faculties still had significant control over their own governance, as was the case in Norway, Portugal and in Hungary, many of the issues at stake could not be resolved by executive intervention, because faculties often simply refused to comply.

[Portugal] Sometimes there is… a wall that we cannot climb over. And we have to take extreme measures and go to higher levels of the university to get things [done] which ought to be easily resolved at lower levels of authority… And sometimes problems can't even be solved at higher levels. Because the university is divided into schools, and the schools have independence and having that independence they are able to make some adjustments themselves… And they can always devise some excuses to bend the law and arrange [things the way they want them]. Some problems are resolvable, and some problems are not. We just have to deal with it. (25)

In Norway, the president of the student organization at a recently merged university argued that 'it's easy to get power, but it's hard to give it away'. (26) He went on to explain that within his university, struggles between those who have been vested with new powers and those who were used to having a say in their own governance have led to stalemates in decision-making. In his opinion, most problems emerged – including in the Student Parliament – because the formerly independent university colleges were not able to adjust to the post-merger balance of participation in the governance of their now merged institution.

Student representation at faculties and departments

Across all countries and universities, students had representatives at departmental and faculty levels, and were often able to achieve more there, especially regarding the structure of their study programmes, the organization of teaching and/or exams as well as the choice of pedagogical approaches to be employed in the classrooms. While these local representative student bodies were always integrated with and consulted by the university's umbrella student organization, they did not always have formal voting rights in their institution's central student body. For example, in Norway they joined the student parliament's meetings, but they could not vote; in Germany they were basically run separately from the institutional organization; in Portugal their role and integration varied based on the institution and on the type of student organization; in Hungary they could be integrated within the central student organization, but actual practice regarding representation and voting varied greatly across universities, and even across faculties.

While the key issues raised and fought for by student organizations varied across countries and between successive generations of student leaders, one overarching theme that was always on student leaders' agendas was the quality of teaching and supervision: the nature and content of teaching, the use of digital technologies in classrooms, lecture capture, flexibility in teaching and examination schedules, more individualized supervision and guidance, less standardization across academic disciplines and across examination processes, and reduced student numbers for lectures (in some cases 600–700 students were enrolled in a single course).

> [Norway] The rector and the board are very focussed on institutional autonomy, so the faculties can choose themselves whether they want to distribute information [online], or capture lectures, everything they can just decide themselves… And we think that's maybe the wrong understanding of what institutional autonomy is, because giving students information about how to get their Master degree is part of the university's task – something they have to do. It's not part of the autonomy of the faculty not to give information… The other day, I was looking for some names, and I found a page that had not been updated for five years. It was the names of students who were no longer at the university, and that's quite common… And some [professors] have PowerPoints with whole pages of just text, which is not how PowerPoint is supposed to be used… I once had a Swedish lecturer; there was Swedish text on his PowerPoint, he was speaking in English, and I was thinking in Norwegian… (27)

These issues mattered not only because students felt that the quality of their education suffered but also because in all countries a majority of the student body had to take paid employment while studying to manage the costs of their education. Thus, it was very common that students felt pressed for time and were stressed because of the expectations in the employment market. However, most student organizations argued that it was almost impossible to achieve consensus on such matters within the university because students' interests clashed with those of state policymakers, institutional executives and the academic community. According to student representatives, state officials and university leadership were concerned with budgets, while academics felt overwhelmed, overworked, burnt out and were less concerned with teaching than they were with their research agendas.

> [Portugal] We have a lot of frustrated professors because they have to do both research and teaching. And some want to do one thing, and some want to do the other… Most of the time I was having classes and feeling [that professors] do not want to be here teaching this. And that's bad because we do not get the best experience, and neither do they. We need to find a balance: motivated people giving classes, enough people giving classes, and having a good ratio between students and professors. We also need to have

> motivated researchers that are doing good research and know that they do not have to stop [the research] because they must go and give classes next semester and get frustrated because they have to do that. (28)

While institutions had varying degrees of control over their student numbers, for years it has been commonly felt among student leaders that there is significant pressure from state bodies to increase student numbers without increasing resources. Students frequently spoke out against this, as they felt that this could further degrade the quality of teaching and learning. However, their voice rarely seemed to matter. Priorities were mostly set by national and regional policy agendas and institutional budgetary concerns.

> [Portugal] The professors are not as prepared as they should be... I think it's a national issue... What we are facing now is that too little money is being given to higher education, to development, to innovation... we are facing a moment of stagnation: universities are not hiring as many teachers as they should. They are not improving the quality of infrastructure, and the national government has also been too guilty in this matter. (29)

> [Germany] The mayor... pushed the agenda that this city should be one of Germany's leading science and innovation cities, and you can't have a leading science and innovation city without a strong university of technology. [But instead of saying that] OK, our university of technology needs more money in order to expand, [they said] we need to expand [our student numbers]. Well, that's one agenda, and the other is that German politicians always try to push student numbers, [to be able] to say that Germany is an academic state because we have a complex, multi-layered system which other countries don't have, [even though] they have a much higher nominal academization rate... So, our vice-president for teaching has his own strategy for getting more students to come; he actually wants to try stuff like [lifelong learning]. (30)

Student organizations and their funding

Our data revealed that, to be effective, student organizations needed to have stable and transparent financial backing. With the exception of Norway, it was obvious that this need was not being met in our case study countries. Even in places where this was formally the situation, such as in the UK, student union representatives still did not feel they had secure finances. Part of the reason for this was the lack of transparency that surrounded many student unions' funding arrangements with their universities.

This situation was further aggravated by the fact that across all five of our case study countries, student organizations' membership fees were insufficient. This made student organizations highly dependent on state and university funding, significantly impacting on what they were able to achieve and how far their representative powers went.

Thus, a major difference among countries was the nature of the funding supporting student organizations. This impacted student organizations' ability to lobby leadership and advocate various issues. Our data showed that when the amount of the student organization's income was not guaranteed by law or did not come from funds external to the university, student unions always felt the heat when they tried to raise delicate issues with university leadership.

> [England] In the UK, every university has to have a student union, that's in the law. What the law doesn't say is how much block grant they have to give you, or how much support, those sorts of things… I mean, we could be really controversial and say [to students] don't complete the National Student Survey and do loads of things that the university don't want [students to do], but we probably couldn't guarantee [university] funding the next year for all our staff members and for the work that we do. So that kind of ties into why maybe sometimes we aren't as argumentative. But we still do hold the university to account. (31)

As became clear from some of our UK student union presidents' accounts, there was also a widespread culture of caution and fear among student union leaders. This feeling was not necessarily the result of direct confrontations; it was rather perpetuated by what a student union president described as her interactions being characterized by a suffocating culture of politeness – meaning implicit, but active silencing – leading her to be overly guarded in what she dared to say to senior university administrators.

> [England] I have a weekly meeting with the provost of student experience, where we can kind of air our worries… but because we are in such an overly cautious type of environment, you do feel too rude to say it. I felt myself holding myself back… because you don't want to damage a relationship

> between yourself and the university because you know that we are so reliant on the university. For example, I did bring up diversity of council membership. I've brought it up a couple of times, but each time I say it I can see the vice-chancellor getting angrier and angrier, like 'we've tried, we've tried'. And it's just like 'you haven't tried enough, have you?' But you can't say that because you don't want to damage that relationship when it's kind of like don't bite the hand that feeds you: they are the ones that give us our block grant, our facilities. So, it makes it very hard to be able to express all the truthness in what you want to say, because you are scared of what the repercussions may be for your successor… then they'll be put in a worse situation where students won't get as much of a voice because it's not what the university wants to hear. (32)

Even in Norway, where funding was not perceived to be an issue, the student organizations told us that they refrain from raising controversial issues with the rector when they need to negotiate budgets or ask for more money. This emphasized how – even when conditions are seen to be close to 'ideal' – student unions can feel vulnerable and powerless under the implicit threats of possible financial 'punishments'.

> [Norway] I think the week we applied for extra money for a seminar I wouldn't go to the newspapers criticizing [the leadership of our university] that week. But I never take into consideration that we get our money from the university. But we also have a very good dialogue with the rector and his leadership group, so I think with the friendly tone that we have it wouldn't be a problem… But if we want something and that would be like a huge benefit for us, then we would perhaps work for that, and not criticize them for other things in that period of time… So, it's more about priorities… just picking your battles. (33)

There was also a great variety in the amount of money available to student unions for managing their activities. In Norway, the union was well funded and – if the expenses were justified – additional funds could be requested from the university, as well as from the national government. In Hungary, a portion of the student council's budget was written into law. Therefore, student housing and scholarships did not need to be negotiated within institutions on a yearly basis. However, the operational budget for all other activities was decided by a negotiation between the student council, the university chancellor, and the academic senate.

[Hungary] I negotiate part of the student union's budget with the university's chancellor. We sit down with each other, and I say 'I planned this. On the other hand, you sent a recommendation that's not enough'. [He then tells me that what we asked for] is a lot. Let's agree in the middle. And it's always in the middle. (34)

In Portugal, some student unions had no funding at all. One way they raised cash was by organizing one or two major student events (e.g. graduation ceremonies) where they sold tickets. Other unions received a yearly block grant from their universities, but each year they needed to renegotiate the amounts.

[Portugal] The student unions at the faculties have an annual budget that comes from the government, from the Secretary of State for Sports and Youth that is under the Ministry of Science, Technology, and Higher Education... Because we are a regional student union – an umbrella organization for several local university student unions – we do not get access to that support, so we are mainly self-funded. In May, we have a big event to celebrate the end of the degrees for many students. It's almost like a festival, for one week, and we get our income from that, and it gives us money to work during the whole year and do all the things we do... We also have access to a very small part of a twenty thousand euros pot at universities, so we do not get all of the twenty thousand euros, and that represents less than one per cent of our budget, so it's a very little amount of our annual budget. Universities, meaning all of the higher education institutions that are represented by our students, give us help in some projects with buildings... but not in any other ways because they have their own students to support. (35)

In the UK, universities either gave a block grant to their student unions or allocated their funding as a fixed proportion of a university's budget or pro rata to student numbers. However, since these arrangements were not regulated by national laws or university statutes, the amount could vary year on year, and – according to student union representatives – could also be taken away or arbitrarily reduced.

There were also major differences in the ways student organization officers were remunerated for their work and how much time they were able to allocate for organizational matters. This, in turn, greatly impacted on how efficient they could be in their posts and how much time they were able to allocate to day-to-day university issues, as well as to networking and lobbying to increase the student organization's outreach and influence. In some countries, such as Portugal and Germany, this was an unpaid/voluntary position, and had to be undertaken in addition to maintaining an active student status by attending classes and passing exams.

> [Portugal] My position is all volunteer. All for free. No salaries involved. But I have to study, and do the management of the student union [at the same time]. It is a little too hard. I have to skip many classes. I try to [go to classes] along with my colleagues, and my friends can help me out sometimes. They can lend me some course material, but many times... I just do the exams. I skip all the classes. (36)

In Hungary, the position of student officers was voluntary and had to be done in addition to their studies. But student council leaders received a study fellowship, the amount of which was decided by the student council leadership. The amount of this scholarship varied across universities and in our sample both interviewees told us that they exercised self-restraint and allocated themselves scholarship amounts that were in line with the other study scholarships in their universities. However, they also recounted stories about some student unions voting for excessively high fellowships (three or four times the amount of the average study scholarship). In Norway and the UK student officers were given a paid sabbatical year.

> [Norway] This is not a nine to four job. It's far more. So, the school puts your studies on pause, and you work full-time for the students, and when you finish, they just un-pause it and you start up again. So, I will have to finish my third year when I am not doing student politics anymore. I can be re-elected for two years. This is my second term. But if I wanted to, I could go back to studying one year and then I could become the head of the student union again. I'll probably finish my studies finally after four years. It's a long time... I've had a lot of fun. I've done a lot of good for students. I've grown a lot as a person, but it's about time to finish my studies. (37)

Student organizations and the governance of student welfare issues

One of the most important differences between countries was in the management tasks that student organizations undertook. These, in turn, greatly influenced the weight they carried within formal university governance and the variety of management roles they could fulfil across different university bodies. For example, the fact that in Norway and Hungary student organizations had additional responsibilities linked to student welfare (e.g. managing student housing, bursaries, other campus services for students etc.) increased the weight their views carried in other university committees, senates and governing bodies as well.

In Norway, managing student welfare issues – including housing, childcare, mental health, sports, culture and canteens – was the sole responsibility of the students. All these functions were run on a nonprofit basis by the Student Welfare Organization (SWO). This was an organization whose existence and funding were guaranteed by law. While it was independent from Student Parliaments, it was also governed by students, with the majority of its board being composed of students. The university's leadership could nominate two members to the board, and Student Parliaments could also nominate one or two representatives to the SWO's board. Concomitantly, the SWO board's chair participated in the Student Parliament's monthly meetings and was invited to the most important executive and board meetings within the university, ensuring that there was good communication and collaboration across the university, and between student organizations. Financial support was also provided by state and university block grants, and in-kind support – in the form of land and buildings – from universities and local councils.

> [Norway] I think it could be difficult to understand, because the SWO in one way is a corporation, but in another way is not a corporation. It's so different; that's why it has its own law… We are doing corporate activities, but the aim is not the profit-making. I think that's the most important part to understand, and that we are there for the students, to provide for their welfare. For instance,… we have the main student union, called the Student Parliament. And we also have smaller unions that can freely establish themselves… And for them too, we can fund activities. We can fund smaller student groups. This is also part of [student] welfare… Everything we do is for students, both on an individual level, but also at an organizational level… It's not like in the UK, where they could… invite corporations to come and start their business on campus. [In Norway] we will provide everything students need on campus, for the best market price. It's always supposed to be a price that students can pay for housing, nursery, and food, while most

> health offerings are free. The kindergarten costs are all on the students level. We always have the student in mind. For instance, if there is a child that's sick while the parent is supposed to have an exam, then we can provide a special service... one person can drive out and pick up the child, and bring it to the kindergarten, or they can open the kindergarten early. Our service is unique and [very human centred]. (38)

In none of our other case study countries could we find the equivalent of Norway's SWO. Elsewhere, while some of these student welfare activities were managed by university central bodies or run in consultation and/or collaboration with student unions, other activities – such as food, childcare and sometimes even student housing – were often left to the market to sort out. Hence the variations across countries in how much oversight student bodies could exert over such matters. For example, in Hungary state-subsidized student accommodation in university dormitories was distributed through the student union. State-funded scholarships were also allocated through student unions. It was the same for student entertainment and cultural programmes. However, other issues of student welfare were not in their remit.

> [Hungary] In Hungary, whatever is related to the students is decided by students. For example, how we use scholarships, who we want to reward, and through what reward system. This is up to us to decide. The distribution of housing in student halls is best left in students' hands. Obviously, it's complemented with all kinds of university structures. We aren't the ones managing the actual financial payment system because we need a person who has financial education. But having those decisions here – I don't even understand why this is any different elsewhere, in other countries. (39)

In the UK, the situation varied across institutions but almost all universities provided student accommodation in halls of residence or apartments, although none could provide for their total student population. Although most universities claimed that their student accommodation was run on a nonprofit basis, students frequently felt that the costs were nevertheless prohibitively high. Part of the reason for this was that unlike in many of the continental European countries, UK student housing costs were not subsidized by the state. While universities sometimes offered subsidies, they often only made additional funding available if student unions strongly pushed for it. Such negotiations took students into the centre of university governance.

> [Scotland] Last year we had a lot of campaigning around rent reduction for on-campus, university-owned student accommodation, because basically a lot of students felt that the rent was too high, and it was unmanageable to pay… The previous [student union] president secured an accommodation enhancement fund; and [students now] can apply for that pot of money and basically it can subsidize the rent on campus… it's to help [poorer] students pay their rent. So, I think it is really through projects like that that we collaborate, working with the university every single step of the way to try and find smart solutions to help the people who really do need it the most. (40)

> [England] We don't house all our first-year students, which is typically something that universities can promise. And for the past two years the cost of residences has gone up, so… it's expensive. Not compared to private providers across the road, but it's still expensive… There were students saying that they live onsite, but they still must work two jobs, or their loan doesn't even cover their rent entirely.…. I was welfare officer the year before when the price of residences had all gone up by three per cent, and then this year they've gone up a further 2.5 per cent… one thing that's really frustrated me is that I sit on the residential strategy group, which hasn't met in a while, so I'm not sure where this decision was made, and we were promised when they went up last year, that we would be involved in discussion as a student union, and we haven't been, which is really frustrating. (41)

In Portugal and Germany, issues around student welfare and housing were not automatically managed or decided by student organizations, making it necessary for student organizations to raise such issues individually and independently with their universities and the state, and put external pressure on universities to provide such services if or when their budgets allowed. As a result, some of these activities and services were only randomly and inconsistently available at an affordable price and through students' universities.

> [Portugal] Nowadays the biggest issue we have is student accommodation, student housing. The prices are very, very high and the number of the publicly offered rooms/beds are ridiculously low. So, we negotiate over that. We signed a protocol [with the regional government and the university] that

we are building an academic neighbourhood. It will be a housing project. We will build a thousand beds with controlled prices, and hopefully we can help to solve the problem. But it's a major issue right now. (42)

Student inclusion and weight in institutional governance

As we have shown in the previous sections, while we found broad-level formal inclusion of student organizations in institutional governance across all countries, there was also a significant variation in actual day-to-day governance practices within institutions. It is also important to emphasize that despite the huge variety in the fine details, we found that similarities in external pressures – for example, high costs of living, overall high costs of study even when student fees were not high and pressures to find employment in addition to their studies – resulted in similar patterns of the wider student body having neither the time nor the resources to become involved in student affairs.

With Norway being an exception, we also found similarities in the ways in which institutions – and often national-level policymaking as well – failed to provide adequate, transparent and secure funding for student organizations which would allow them to focus – without fear of repercussions – on issues that they've seen as essential for their complete inclusion in shared governance.

This led us to the next important point: except for Norway and to a lesser extent Germany, it was difficult to talk about shared governance in relation to students, because – in actual practice – student leaders were often treated as part of a 'box-ticking' game – the appearance of representation rather than a genuine equal partnership and full participation in institutional conversations and strategic planning. We also found similarities across countries in the ways in which the more informal language of trust and partnership was often used in institutions to disempower students, instead of them being accepted as equal partners in the governing of student affairs.

Because student leaders often perceived that they were only being offered or given perfunctory opportunities for engagement in formal institutional and national governance structures, most student organizations did not think that they had been able to significantly and transformatively influence the direction, the content or the cost of their study experience. Many who had begun their university and student organization experience with high hopes and enthusiasm finished their academic studies with little confidence that either the institution or national-level higher education policymaking had what they saw as their best interests at heart.

The academic community in university governance

There is a growing scholarship on the changing role and loss of influence of the academic community within university governance over the past two decades (Rowlands 2019, Loveday 2018, Park 2013, Blackmore *et al.* 2010, Enders *et al.* 2009). However, to our surprise, in our study, many academics argued that they still felt that they had significant influence in the governance of their institution. While there were significant variations across countries, and even across individual institutions, our data showed that, in this respect only, the situation of academics in the UK was markedly different to that of academics in continental European universities largely because of the routine appointment of external candidates to senior managerial-academic positions. Historically, vice chancellors in the UK were virtually always selected from an external pool of candidates. In the current era, positions for pro-vice-chancellors, deans and department heads also became increasingly 'professionalized' and external candidates were regularly sought in preference to internal candidates. There were relatively high levels of fluctuations across the sector ('job-hopping'), both in top positions and in the ranks of the academic community.

In contrast, in most continental universities where we interviewed, internally elected members of the academic community still held most of the top positions at university, faculty and department levels. Fluctuations in the academic workforce were relatively low compared to the UK, and 'job-hopping' as part of professional advancement was still relatively rare. While executive positions in continental universities were not necessarily held for longer periods of time by the same individuals than was the case in the UK, the senior academics elected internally for these positions regularly returned to their academic posts at the end of their executive tenures. As it will be seen later in this chapter, this made a significant difference in attitudes within the executive. Further, in continental universities academics had strong representation on university and faculty boards/ councils, comfortable majorities on senates, and tended to hold majorities on educational and research committees. Many of these bodies kept their relevance in university governance and managed to avoid being turned into rubber-stamp bodies by the executive, as could be the case in UK universities. Such distributed and multilayered academic representation usually assured that any concentration of power at the top of institutions was somewhat counterbalanced by strong lateral structures at faculty and departmental levels.

Nevertheless, our data also clearly indicated that – despite their significant and often decisive weight in institutional self-governance – academics working in continental universities often had similar grievances to those of academics working in UK universities. They worried about changes in state regulation of higher education, changes to the amount and structure of funding, increasing levels of precarity and casualization, unmanageable workloads, lack of research time, the often limited nature of the research inquiries they were able to conduct, the push for competition and marketization under the guises of impact, societal engagement and innovation; and the impact of all these processes on the quality of teaching and research.

In the following two sections, we will focus on academics in senior executive positions and on the governance of teaching, as these are two of the key areas through which the everyday practices of academic governance, and the potential weight and influence of academic communities within institutional governance could be observed. It is important to emphasize that there is great diversity not only across countries and between individual institutions but often even between departments of the same university.

Academics in senior executive positions – the manager-academics

In continental universities, appointing external candidates to senior leadership positions through competitive external calls is no longer as uncommon as it once was. However, it is still significantly more common to have internally nominated candidates elected directly by the university's staff and students; in some institutions, the election of the rector happens via the mediation of a university council/board. On these councils/boards – in addition to external members – academics, administrative staff and students continue to have strong representation. As one of our Hungarian ex-rector interviewees explained:

> [Hungary][Appointing external candidates] is not the practice here. It is always a candidate from the inside… [Inviting external candidates] has never happened… [In rectoral elections] competitiveness is quite limited. There aren't too many candidates. Usually, it is always two candidates… And the candidates can come from different faculties, but at this university [the rector always comes from] the three most prestigious faculties… It is customary that the previous rector takes the responsibility of nominating the next candidate, or candidates… (43)

The above also highlights that in continental universities – in addition to the formal governance regulations and statutes – there were unwritten customary practices that assured things were done as they had always been done within institutions. In Hungary, two examples of many such unwritten practices included asking outgoing leaders to nominate new internal candidates and giving high-prestige and influential faculties greater weight in leadership contests. While the standing power of such unwritten practices varied across countries and universities, our data indicated that they were common beyond Hungary as well. As an academic in a large Norwegian research university argued:

> [Norway] I've worked on faculty-wide committees, and representatives from the bigger units definitely make clear that we are the 'junior people'. I mean, they would never say it out loud, but you get the clear message through other means that they have all the big student numbers, and they are the ones with these huge MA programmes. (44)

It was also suggested that such informal practices were only rarely challenged or changed, which brought long-term stability to institutional governance, but – sometimes – tensions as well. A senior academic in the executive group of his faculty in a Norwegian university discussed the tensions in his own workplace as follows:

> [Norway] We have a huge… conflict in our faculty now, regarding graduate education… So, we asked to have discussions… at the faculty level. And our

faculty dean, who has been in her post since 2005, [longer than our rector], said 'well, we can include some of your requests within our framework, but [the key issues are not up for negotiation], that's out of the question'... And then this issue comes to the rector, where a professor from our department... says in a meeting with the rector that they have problems with this dean, [because] she is not listening... And the rector shows a lot of support for the people experiencing these problems, but then... somehow the informal thing... makes addressing the problems very difficult... and so nothing changes. (45)

Academics holding these leadership positions tended to return to their tenured (professorial) posts within their own universities once their executive positions came to an end. This often made academics more wary of the changes they implemented during their time in the post, as these could have lasting impacts not only on the lives of their long-time colleagues and friends but also on their own working conditions. However, their safe positions within the institution also gave them more confidence to act, when needed. As one of our rector interviewees argued in Portugal:

[Portugal] [The general council of the university] elects the rector... and they also have the power to put me on the street... [But I am a professor in this university and] it's very difficult for a professor to lose his position. Actually, the professors have all the power in the world in their offices, so it's almost impossible to fire a professor. (46)

Thus, the emergence of a so-called professional academic leadership class that moved from high-level position to high-level position across higher education institutions and national borders – a practice well established in much of the English-speaking higher education world – seemed to be still in its infancy in continental Europe. In our sample of nine continental universities, we found only one university where the rector was an external 'professional'. However, both in Norway and in Germany, laws and institutional regulations often made it possible for universities to appoint externally the heads of schools and departments. Such appointments, in turn, strengthened top-down decision-making lines within continental institutions, giving more power to rectors over heads of departments and faculties, and to heads of departments over their staff. However, many academics opposed the shift to such a system exactly because they felt that it resulted in an upward centralization of power. Our data indicated that it was still relatively rare for academic communities to decide to put such rules into practice, even when part of a department or faculty thought that an external candidate could be a better option. The statements below illustrate the different points of view:

> [Germany] In our Land, you can actually have both systems: you can have [the elected dean], or you can have a professional [appointed] dean... But our department decided to have an elected dean... What some universities do, and faculties who have a professional dean, they usually appoint somebody from outside that does not come from the faculty... Because [elected heads] are usually the older colleagues and this is the last step in their careers, and after four years, eight years, whatever, they retire... And I think it's better if you come from outside and see the faculty from [the point of view of an] outsider as opposed to spending an entire career on this faculty, and then taking this very powerful position and not being able to independently see the faculty. And so, this is why, all faculties that I know, hired somebody from outside because they were afraid of all the internal connections. (47)

> [Norway] In our university, there are people who are eager for more appointed positions... and so we have an appointed head in most of the departments of the faculty... I have never been in favour of that... because that means that those appointees support the line of the dean and the head of department, because the head of department has been appointed by the dean, so they will more often look upwards rather than downwards... There have been a few examples of departments that want to go back to the head of department being elected... [because they had a] very bad experience with an appointed head, and they felt that the appointed head was not attentive enough to what was going on in the department. (48)

The professionalization of leadership structures in continental universities was instead achieved by putting in place and expanding parallel support systems, in which financial directors, human relations officers and other high-level administrative staff facilitated and complemented the work of the academic community. As explained in Chapter 3, such parallel administrative structures might have been able to exercise varying degrees of power, but – except for

Hungary – administrative-professional staff, for the most part, had largely oversight and advisory roles and were rarely able to override decisions taken by the academic community. An interview with the financial head of a large regional university in Norway highlights these points:

> [Norway]
>
> Q *Do you have any decision-making power?*
> A I wish I had it, but I don't. I have a dialogue with the deans, concerning their strategy and their priorities concerning the budgets, and I can give my recommendations, and I do that with the rector and to the board. But I don't decide; that's up to the rector and the board. (49)

In Portugal, according to the head of administration in a large research university, there had been some recent attempts to increase the power of the centre within universities. However, even after significant changes to the overall administrative structures of some of their large research universities – a few universities transitioned from public to foundation universities – the balance of powers remained tilted towards the academic community and the deans:

> [Portugal] It was very difficult for our rector, and it is still difficult now, but less than in the past... This new, unified, and centralized foundation system helped the rector to have more power, an additional power, which is crucial for having strategic planning. Because in the old system, [where faculties were completely independent of the centre], it was impossible to have strategic planning. If the deans didn't believe in that plan of action, [it was impossible to implement it]. (50)

In contrast to continental universities, in the UK, the concentration of power in the hands of vice chancellors and their executive teams significantly increased during the past decade. For most such positions – including school heads and deans – candidates were generally recruited externally from a pool of international candidates. The turnover in most such positions was high; every few years a new external candidate was recruited who reshuffled structures at university and/or faculty/school level. While there was variety across types of institutions, leadership structures in older research universities were more stable than in newer teaching-oriented institutions. The extreme situation described by an internationally recruited dean, who moved from continental Europe to a UK university, may not be typical but may not be uncommon in a significant part of the higher education sector in the UK:

> [UK] In a move for greater accountability... [our governance] ends up being a very top-down structure. [In our university] there were no governance structures that included staff... and I was told that that is characteristic of a modern university... [At academic board meetings] there wasn't dialogue about things, it wasn't a decision-making process. You could raise questions, but it was chaired by the vice-chancellor... and part of the business was an accounting that the board of governors had reviewed proposals for the latest restructure. There was no documentation that went with that... the conversation was done entirely with the board of governors and the vice chancellor's group, and then the deans were notified. [The other deans and I said that] we are probably going to be made to do this, so let's talk about different restructures that were possible... [We made our suggestions] but then we were told that well, they had their own model. They didn't accept any of our models, and they are going forward with theirs... And then the VC, a month later, did a series of presentations to the whole staff saying this is what we are doing and it's to save money... And the staff were completely unconvinced that they'd save money, because with the last restructure they'd saved no money and in fact they had spent more money... But it was pushed down by deans, associate deans, learning and teaching directors, research directors, and then those people got taken out of the system, and new people got put in who had no history with the institution. So, at the end of the restructure, only one person was a dean who had been a dean before. (51)

One major difference we found across the sector was the level of academic mobility. Our data indicated that academic mobility was highest in the UK, while in Hungary and Portugal there was almost none at all. However, even in the UK, academic mobility depended on type of institution: in smaller, teaching-oriented regional institutions staff mobility was lower than across research intensive and Russell group institutions, or the universities located in London and large regional urban centres. The lack of stability and continuity revealed in the above UK quotation is in stark contrast to the experiences of academics in continental universities, where people often spent their entire academic lives in the same institution at which they started their graduate studies. Their colleagues were often their former professors or students, and they were long-time friends. This also meant that the feeling that 'we are all in the same boat' was often more prevalent. One of the department heads in a Portuguese university gave an example:

> [Portugal] Since January, I'm the head of my department, and I am not obliged to teach. But I do teach half loads because human resources are very scarce in our university, and as department head I cannot ask my colleagues to make an extra effort if I myself do not step forward. So that's why I continue teaching. (52)

Similarly in Norway, an internationally recruited junior academic told us:

> [Norway] People stick around here; there's very little fluctuation actually. I think in our department we've had one person leave, and that's sort of the only story in known memory. So, I think the fact that they hired as many foreigners as they recently have, also in permanent positions, it might change that a bit... but in our department there is definitely an expectation that we will be around for quite a while. (53)

This suggests that in many continental universities not much has changed in the decade that passed since Musselin's 2004 study on the European academic labour market, which concluded that 'One can expect international careers to primarily include a few top academics. Most others, and especially young candidates, still develop national careers' (2004: 73).

The academic community and the governance of teaching

One important area where we found major differences across countries was in the governance of teaching. The ways academics were able to start a new academic programme, module or course, or make modifications to existing courses, usually depended both on external – national and regional – regulations and on internal processes put in place by academics' own institutions. On paper, the system seemed to be the most rigid in Portugal, where government regulations restricted expenditure on new courses and programmes, and the Agency for Assessment and Accreditation of Higher Education had the power to restrict the freedom of institutions when they tried to set up new study programmes. A senior academic in Portugal told us:

> [Portugal] There is a constraint from the government… that says that each year we cannot increase overall salary expenditures [higher than the average of] the previous three years… So, we're basically looking to existing staff if we want to open [new programmes], and looking very much for synergies between different programmes… So, we are trying to use courses that are already running in other programmes, and having a good mix with some new courses that people are very interested in teaching. (54)

A faculty dean in arts and sciences in Portugal framed the issue this way:

> [Portugal Ten years ago, we didn't have an accreditation agency, so we used to direct our programmes in a more informal way. [We implemented the Bologna Process in 2007] and now we need to present results to be evaluated, and assessment to be integrated in a lot of formal structures… We need to submit the proposal [to the Agency for Assessment and Accreditation of Higher Education], and it's a very complex form to fill in with… lots of justifications to defend the need for that programme. This level of justification is necessary primarily because, at the moment, the government doesn't allow lots of programmes in the same fields, if [they think that] the needs of the market do not align [with the programme offerings]. (55)

In Hungary, as in Portugal, national-level financial and quality assurance regulations were a concern for departments and universities. In addition, over the past decade, the government reduced and restructured the Hungarian Accreditation Committee's (HAC) budget and introduced an additional step in the process: while initially accreditation was a bilateral process, taking place only between universities and the accreditation committee, in the mid-2000s a ministry-level Education Office was established with powers to validate all accreditation decisions, and – on occasion – overturn them. From that time on, universities had to apply to the Education Office for accreditation, not to the HAC directly, and it was the Education Office which, in turn, contracted the HAC directly. According to one of the officers from the Education Office, this 'mediated' accreditation protocol made quality assurance processes more centralized, but also gave it control of the process independently of the Accreditation Committee:

> [Hungary] In 1993 we created this independent quality assurance body, the Hungarian Accreditation Committee (HAC). The objective was to meet academic expectations. It was the first ever external validation of [university] course programmes. Thus, for all institutional accreditations that took place between 1993 and 2002… the law said that we should go back and repeat this [institutional and] programme accreditation every five years. While institutional accreditation is going well, programme accreditation [cannot be paid for from] the state-funding we provided for the HAC… Basically, HAC can now run programme accreditation… only if we [the Education Office at the Ministry], provide the support, because HAC has no resources; we have significantly reduced the state budget available to them as an independent organization. (56)

These changes in the law prompted universities occasionally to challenge HAC's decisions, especially when universities had direct contacts to the ministry. As a senior university administrator in a large regional research university argued during our interview:

> [Hungary] If the Minister has the right to authorize a degree program, we will try to ask for help, even if the program is not supported by the Hungarian Accreditation Committee… This does not mean that we will not deliver quality. However, right now we are unable to do so. For example, at present, in Hungary, it is not possible to start certain types of special needs education programs because there are no academics in Hungary who are qualified to teach them according to the HAC rules. But there is a demand for this, and we cannot afford the luxury of not applying and lobbying for it. This would be a win-win situation because it will be good for the university, good for the region, good for the children who need it. (57)

In contrast, in Norway and Germany, external national-level accreditation processes – once certain quality assurance structures were put in place at institutional level – allowed for a more relaxed approach, with many universities having significant powers to control their programme and course offerings. An external board member in a large research university in Norway reported:

> [Norway] If the Norwegian Agency for Quality Assurance in Education (NOKUT) accredited you as a university you can sort of create your own programmes... [We do have to have a quality assurance system in place that is approved by NOKUT, where we explain how]... the different parts of the university impact on quality assurance, for example programme coordinators, head of the institute, dean, and what kind of role does the dean have in the quality system. All the roles have to be defined in relation to each other, and on their own, and they have to have a system for [internal] accreditation, and a system for continuance, [on the ways that] different study programmes can be modified... We also have to have routines for when you want to terminate a programme... So, the board knows about it and can implement it.... These things are not at faculty level. Decisions are made by... the [internal] Education Quality Committee... and all large changes to a programme have to go through that committee, and then the committee recommends that it be accredited. Then the board rubber stamps the documents... They get all the documents, but I don't know if they actually read them. I think they trust that the... committee has done the work. (58)

An academic in a German technical university said:

> [Germany] If you would like to launch a new study programme... you have two directions: I would discuss it with the dean, who is responsible for teaching in your own department [and] faculty... to find out if they are interested and if they see potential there. Right after, or even in parallel, you talk with the pro-rector of the university who is involved with teaching... on both levels the best case would be [that they] say OK, we are interested, and we see potential in this at faculty level. Let's go for it. On the other side – from those who have the bigger picture and strategy for the university – they would say OK, that also fits into our big picture, we would like to get more involved in this direction. Let's go for it. These would be the best outcomes. (59)

Our findings indicate that for what is termed 'classroom autonomy' – the freedom to teach what you want once you close the door of your classroom – the leadership style of a university and its schools/faculties was often more important than the external restrictions placed on the institutions. This is exemplified by the very different experiences of two UK junior academics, quoted below, one working in a teaching-focused institution and the other in a large research university. The first reported:

> [UK] The idea of subject communities has been something that's been pushed quite a lot. We've now had leaders in those roles, so we have a head of department... [and] each department has separate subject communities within it. Each of those subject communities has a head of that cluster who looks after a cluster of courses. So, in terms of the university, I think we've gained autonomy within that structure. Externally, in terms of governance and so on, it's still bounded by all of the Quality Assurance Agency (QAA) procedures and the benchmarking statements and so on... I've been in a course where we have always been either building the initial two courses or validating an additional one... So, we've always been striving and building. I haven't been ever in the position that I parachuted into something that's already up and going. (60)

On the other hand, the second told a different story:

> [UK] On the teaching and learning forum, I'm the youngest one. I've only just joined, but it's already been very clear that they probably don't want me there. [They are] dismissive of anything that I suggest, which is what I mean about ageism generally, you know.... So there's that thing of just not being taken seriously, I think, because of my age. I mentioned it to somebody and was told that I'd get taken seriously when I had children. [And] I do think it's across the board; I've talked to quite a few junior academics who have pretty much had the same experiences. (61)

In stark contrast to the second quotation, in another UK research-focused university, a senior academic argued that academic staff in his department had a lot of freedom to develop their own teaching content and styles. However, a strong caveat in his argument was – and this came up across most universities in the UK – that nowadays it was not enough for academics to make a compelling scientific argument to justify their teaching suggestions; they had to be able to also make a viable business case, convincing the senior executive that their idea was not going to lose money for the department and the university:

> [UK] At our department we give a lot of academic freedom to staff; we give them room to grow, develop new ideas, take ownership of their new ideas. So, if I have a member of staff coming to me… I want them to make a business case at the back of their minds, and an academic case at the back of their minds. [They need to be able to] describe why this idea is fascinating intellectually, and how we will not lose money achieving it… Then we have groups of specialists… and they need to discuss the idea within the group. But, I don't want the group to be able to block ideas, so even if there is not necessarily agreement, I'm happy to allow something to grow and be tested. And then you have to go through a school process… And then you have to go to the university board. And sometimes there are issues there, but I haven't seen anything being blocked. (62)

In Portugal and Hungary, changing academic programmes and sometimes even individual courses is a difficult and lengthy process where even relatively small changes (e.g. replacing a couple of mandatory courses) required going first to education committees in departments, faculties, the central university bodies, such as the senate and the senior management as well as the financial management at each level. Only after internal approval at all these levels was it possible to submit an application to the Agency for Assessment and Accreditation of Higher Education in Portugal or the Accreditation Committee in Hungary. However, in both countries it was relatively rare to initiate major changes to programmes or establish completely new modules and programmes. In Portugal, one of the main reasons was that once a new programme had been started, it was almost impossible to terminate. As a senior academic in Portugal argued, this made university central management very cautious:

> [Portugal] I think we have a cultural problem: it is very hard to start new things, even to just have them approved in our internal government bodies… because it's also very hard to kill a program. So, I think that we don't take risks, because we know that once a program starts no one will ever say this was a failure, let's stop it. It's very, very hard. (63)

When starting a new programme in Portugal – partly because of the austerity hiring freeze – universities very rarely employed new staff. As a result, most new programmes in the universities where we interviewed had been started as joint academic courses established between two or more universities. This not only spread the costs across more institutions but also led to positive collaborations across the sector, reducing competition between universities. Thus a senior academic in a regional university in Portugal told us:

> [Portugal] We offer a Master's degree with another university. We also have another one with a polytechnic institute… These are joint MA degrees, and also short degree courses… [There are] several reasons [for starting such collaborations]. I believe we wanted to cooperate anyway, but it was also necessary because of the specialization of the staff… So… the director of this course was, for example, in another university, and the staff was located at both institutions. In another degree program the director is from our school, and the staff [are from other institutions]. [The other reason was] the students, I mean in terms of the number of students, they count for each institution… It's a strong argument… Of course, the financial aspect of sharing resources, staff resources, is also… important for the university… Public universities in this country are dealing with austerity… There are many things we can't do because there isn't enough money. (64)

In Hungary, the chancellor system has had a significant impact on the educational side of the university. Chancellors were able to introduce hiring freezes, force departments to make staff redundant, force academics to teach more courses and cut academic research time by hiring fewer lecturers and not adjusting or reducing teaching structures to reflect the dwindling numbers of existing staff. Then, out of necessity, adjustments and reductions were often undertaken by the departments themselves. As a senior academic in a large research university explained:

> [Hungary] The chancellor doesn't have the right to shut down a programme. It's only the rector that can say that now I want to shut down this programme, and I want to fire [the academic staff]… Of course, the chancellor can apply informal pressure. He can allocate less money to the faculties… Last year one of our faculties – which is very unprecedented – had to fire twenty or thirty people, professors… because there was a deficit in the budget… The chancellor required these kinds of measures, to cut the number of professors. But actually, what was done is that… those professors who were not very good professors and were at least sixty-five – maybe twelve or fifteen

professors – they were asked to retire... and then there were approximately eight or nine professors who actually were active, who were fired. But those people were fired based on their scholarly achievement: they didn't publish articles; they didn't do research. (65)

However, both in Portugal and Hungary strict external formal rules and regulations still left room for initiative inside the classroom. Because of this the majority of our interviewees argued that, in their teaching practices, they had significant autonomy and claimed that this kind of freedom was among the reasons that they were still in the profession. Even for junior academics, as one of our interviewees in Hungary argued, there was plenty of autonomy and freedom within the classroom:

[Hungary]

Q *If you see that a course does not work well and you think you should change the content, is it a very complicated and cumbersome process to do so?*
A Well, if you want to do it formally. But that doesn't stop me from just writing it into the course curriculum, teaching new literature in the following semester or trying out a new methodology... I don't know whether it's allowed or not, but I do it. Hundreds of specialist literature and better research and results are coming, so it doesn't prevent me from putting them into the next semester, or even right away. [In terms of grading] everyone marks in whatever way they want to... Nobody is watching, checking, asking. If the student really has the guts, he might report me to the Student Union, but in fact nobody cares. No one cares what I teach in my courses; never during my 4–5 years has anyone come to see what I was doing, what was really happening during my courses. (66)

In the UK, universities retain full autonomy over their teaching. However, issues emerged because of the pressures exerted by the state's policy of marketization. This has increasingly impacted on teaching, particularly in universities heavily dependent on student recruitment where university-wide marketing departments have started to gain broader powers in programme and course evaluations: in such places market considerations can become dominant. Risk assessment and financial viability planning can become factored into academic thinking to such an extent that it conditions course planning and reduces innovation. A senior academic in a regional, teaching-oriented university provided an example:

> [UK] [When starting a new programme or course] you would rely on your market research, and you would also rely on the marketing department in your university... And so... you wouldn't just dream up a lovely thing because [you] were interested in it. [I know it happened in the past that] something was developed around [people's interests]... a masters pathway or something, and then it didn't recruit because students weren't interested. We are not like that anymore, we are much savvier now about 'does the market need this?' (67)

In contrast, in Norway and Germany academics seemed able to shape programmes based entirely on academic-scientific considerations. Thus in the Norwegian universities where we interviewed, we found that academic considerations remained the most important factors in designing undergraduate and graduate study programmes. While broader societal needs were not ignored or dismissed when planning strategic directions for their universities and departments, academics had broad freedoms – supported both by university boards and state actors – to design curricula that provided students with lifelong skills and sound subject knowledge. This also meant that, as one of the external academic board members in a research university argued, universities did not have to discontinue or reduce academic fields and programmes just because there was no immediate 'market' demand for certain subjects:

> [Norway] We have been through a period of time where people have asked for more scientific research in mathematics, ICT, statistics, everything that has to do with technology. So, if you come up with an idea to increase resources in technology-driven issues everybody clapped their hands. But, on the other side, when it comes to the humanities, some people have said, that it's not relevant to business, humanities do not create new jobs, it's not value creation, it's not transformation, it's not helping our competitive edge as a nation. If the structure was very open to those kinds of moods or fashions or signals, we could have destroyed something that is extremely important to our university now, namely the quality in humanities – one of the areas in which we are excelling from a global perspective... So, we listen to the [external] signals, but look at what we are and what we would like to be, and

try to develop what you might call the strengths of our university, somewhat independent of the moods and the fashions… And that is different from a market driven organization. I mean, if you develop toothpaste, you must make toothpaste that people would like to buy tomorrow. So, you must be market driven. But we are not making toothpaste; we are developing competencies. So that's one thing that's positive with the fact that universities are autonomous and not market driven. (68)

In Germany, according to one interviewee, nobody would interfere with an academic's teaching and research plans as long as they did not disturb other colleagues' territories:

[Germany] The main problem, or only problems, arise here if that's an area that somebody is already working on. So, if I would say tomorrow, as a virologist, that I want to work on bacteria tomorrow, I could get the resources and probably also the patient samples to do that. But then my colleague from microbiology wouldn't be very happy about this. So, as long as I stay in the area of virology, nobody would interfere with that. But I also do a lot of work in immunology – the interaction of viruses with the immune system – and we have a chair for immunology here, so if I start something that's very immunology focussed, I usually discuss that with him, and then start this as a collaboration for example. (69)

Thus the picture that emerges across Europe is that the governance of teaching is regulated and directed by multiple internal and external actors at multiple governance levels and that there are many variations between countries and within systems. Our evidence suggests, however, that, with qualifications in individual systems and individual institutions, the decline in academic participation in institutional policymaking has not yet been paralleled in respect to the governance of teaching. Although there are many roadblocks and deterrents to stop academics from designing their subject offerings free from constraints and to be able to close the door and talk freely about their subjects to their students, the governance of teaching still remains essentially in their hands.

5

The Changing Idea and Role of Universities in Europe

Perceived failure of the institution at stake is often seen as the cause of institutional crisis. The institution is perceived as not meeting functional expectations, and lack of performance may also undermine long-standing trust into its normative basis. Developments around the modern university suggest that institutional change may also be caused by institutional success (Olsen 2007). The university has in many ways been a success. Over recent decades, the university has grown enormously, attracting ever more students, extending its research into more and more areas, and being asked to take up more and more roles in contributing to solving socio-economic problems of modern societies. The university has developed into a key institution of the 'knowledge society'. Yet, the university also seems to have become a victim of its success facing work overload, and sometimes raises unrealistic expectations, and competing visions about the idea and role of the university in society.

This chapter reflects on what our study of governance reforms across Europe can tell us about the changing idea and role of the university in Europe. Massification and 'modernization' of higher education are not neutral to the idea and role of the university while explicitly or implicitly carrying ideas and expectations as regards the institutional form of the university.

Ideas and expectations tend to come in packages: models of how a modern higher education system may look like, models of how to run the field of higher education and models of how to assure proper service delivery. Such models tend to perceive the university as a single institution that can be reformed and governed according to some standardized template. The university may, for example, be regarded as a public agency closely aligned to the priorities of the state. The university is an instrument for achieving national goals and expected to follow governmental priorities. Education and research are primarily perceived as an important driver for national wealth or national welfare; the university's roles and development depend on political priorities, governmental regulations and funding that shape its directions. The university as an organization with its hierarchy, rule system and performance measures becomes the main addressee for governmental steering. Autonomy and accountability are two sides of the same coin; some decision-making autonomy is delegated to the university while it is at the same time held accountable for its effectiveness and efficiency in achieving purposes that are set by the state.

The model of the university as a service enterprise embedded in economic competition provides another prominent example. Within this perspective the university is a market actor, and education and research become commodified, goods to be produced and sold. Competition and strategic positioning within the market are key mechanisms that shape organizational success and thus the landscape of higher education. Increasing competition requires rapid organizational responses to ever-changing opportunities and constraints in the market. Strong and professional organizational management and leadership become essential for directing the course of the institution. Management has a responsibility for the university as a whole; it needs to control the university's human and material resources as well as the organization's performance within an ever-changing environment. Ideas and tools from business become popular in running the university as an organization. The university has more autonomy from the state while it also becomes responsible for its own fate within the marketplace.

Obviously, these models stand in contrast to older ideals of the university as a community of scholars based on a long-term social contract with society acknowledging the university as a cultural institution based on academic values and principles. Instead, the new models call for institutional change to overcome this earlier model for which it is believed that reform is necessary to overcome its manifold shortcomings.

The following takes such models as ideal types, as sources of inspiration rather than appropriate descriptions of what is happening. Rather than assuming a single trend and institutional convergence, our research raises the question of whether there are any general trends and whether there is convergence or, as we will argue, some persistent variations in state and university traditions, in the reform of the university as an organization, and in the shaping of the institutional landscape of higher education.

Growth and 'modernization'

Over the last three decades, public-sector reforms have at the face of it aimed at changing the role of the state, the relationship between the state and the public organizations delivering the services, as well as changing the internal governance of these organizations. Governments stepping back from direct steering and tight procedural control, placing public organizations more at arm's length of direct control from political authorities, has been advocated as a way of improving performance in service provisions. It has indeed been widely discussed as to how the role of the state, and its relationship with its public service organizations, is changing, what the implications for their external and internal governance might be and what such changes deliver in terms of expected improvements of public services. A fascinating scholarly debate emerged focusing on the state's apparent loss of its traditional role in steering society and public policy being replaced by a more decentralized form of self-governance and a shift from 'Old Public Administration' to 'New Public Management'.

Higher education in Europe has been no stranger to such political reform attempts and scholarly debates. In recent decades, higher education has experienced unprecedented growth, in quantitative terms in regard to the size of the field and related costs, as well as in qualitative terms related to political and societal expectations. This has in turn triggered policymakers' attention to the field, its functioning and organization. Many of the recent policy initiatives are the result of the tremendous changes that European higher education underwent over the last decades and the need to deal with massification. One of the major features of recent decades has been the persistent expansion of higher education, translated in the growth of enrolments, number and type of institutions, and number and type of programmes. Growth and expansion as well as the search for societal and economic relevance have also affected research. Internationally and nationally, research in higher education has experienced substantive growth. In a self-amplifying cycle of effects, increasing socio-economic demand for research and innovation on the one hand and restless scholarship steadily fashioning more cognitive domains on the other hand have led to research moving out in many directions and to new frontiers. In addition, the rise of 'big science' with its large-scale facilities and huge budgets called for further investment and cooperation to create and maintain 'critical mass'.

The fact that the number of students enrolled in higher education has multiplied several times in a few decades has translated into growing costs, which became a significant issue almost everywhere, and governments have been struggling to find additional funds to sustain and pursue further the process of expansion (Musselin and Texeira 2014). The financial challenge has been further complicated by an adverse financial climate that characterized the public sector during most of the last decades, challenging the sustainability of the traditional financial reliance of higher education on public funding. In consequence, a series of policy changes focused on financial issues that are, however, also effecting the role and idea of the university. First, growth of the field took place, at least partly, via the establishment of less costly new types of higher education institutions which became later known as universities of applied sciences providing shorter educational programmes and being less involved in research. This undermined the ideal that a university is necessarily characterized by being part of both the education system and the research system, both roles benefiting from a teaching-research nexus. Second, further political measures were introduced in search of efficiency and effectiveness in system funding and organizational operations. De-coupling funding for teaching and research, introducing performance-based funding systems and channelling funding into competitively organized allocation mechanisms provide prominent examples. This shift signalled the possible end of the idea that the university deserves financial support because of what it is while it should preferably be funded for what it does and what it achieves.

Educational expansion also had another effect on the idea and role of the university. Social groups that had previously been excluded from elite universities streamed into higher education driven by an ongoing social demand for participation. This development changed the relationship between higher education and socio-economic stratification in society, including the relationship between higher education and the labour market. Traditionally higher education could focus on the social reproduction of elites in society delivering graduates for recruitment into the upper echelons of the labour market. With the rise of high participation systems, universities and a growing number of other providers became involved in a much wider role of socio-economic status distribution among various strata of society. In turn, higher education system design and differentiation became relevant for much wider processes of status distribution, who gets access to what kind of higher education and, from thereon, to which socio-economic life chances, including the maintenance of the traditional elite function of universities.

Moreover, this expansion has been increasingly linked to direct economic motivations and purposes, with the state seemingly explicating an instrumental view as regards higher education and research as a tool for innovation, growth and competitive advantage. The relatively new labels of the knowledge economy and of the knowledge society have become a widespread discourse in which the university plays an important instrumental role. Sure, every economy and society are knowledge-based while the implications of what this self-description of 'modernity' means are potentially far reaching. Following Jessop (2008), a first change concerns a further shift from national macroeconomics towards the economics of the global market. A further change concerns the extension of the economic sphere to include fields and actors that were previously considered as being outside the sphere of the market. A final change involves the expectation of spheres and actors considered as being outside the market to be economically relevant. Higher education figures possibly in all three areas: it is increasingly constructed in post-national, regional, international and global terms and is being reorganized on this basis at various levels; it is increasingly thought of as a directly economic factor (being itself profit-oriented or market-mediated); and, where it is perceived as being outside the market or the quasi-market economy, it may be seen as a factor that is expected to contribute directly to economic competitiveness.

The state and the higher education landscape

General templates for public sector reform, such as New Public Management, seemed to provide scripts for a 'modernization' agenda in search of efficiency, effectiveness and economic contributions in higher education. While New

Public Management comes in different guises, common assumptions are that state-higher education relationships have been changing and that environmental pressures on the field and its institutions have grown. Further, it is assumed that changing regulatory systems, changing resource dependencies and institutional pressures will reshape the organizational configuration of the European university towards the corporate-managerial ideal type.

The grand narrative of change provided by such international policy templates for best practice suggests that governance in higher education would not only have undergone certain substantial shifts in recent decades but would also lead to a trend of policy convergence across countries. Our research was timely for exploring such assumptions for a range of countries across Europe in that it was undertaken at a point when the dust of the political rhetoric had settled. An argument can be made that we observe policy discourses in all countries under observation being influenced by the grand narrative of change, though with different timing and emphasis. Ideas around the role of the university in the knowledge economy or knowledge society, of its important role for innovation and growth and thus for international competitiveness *have been travelling the globe*. Calls for more efficiency and effectiveness in higher education, and for governments stepping back from hands-on control, delegating authority to the institutions can, for example, be found in all European countries that we studied. In other words, we observe some ideational policy convergence inspired by the grand narrative of change that travelled the world during the last decades. In practice, however, things turned out to be somewhat different with persistent and sometime even growing diversity in policymaking.

A first important observation concerns the role of the state in higher education (see Chapter 1). The empirical evidence shows that states not only continue to govern higher education and have not lost any of their policymaking power but have intensified their efforts to shape and re-shape higher education according to their political priorities. What emerges here is that governments play a more significant role in setting the targets for higher education using old and new ways in steering or directing the field and the institutions. State pressures and attempts at external governance have increased, while higher education has become bigger, more expensive, less elitist, politically more visible, and economically more strategic.

At the same time, higher education policies can differ across countries as regards policy beliefs about the idea and role of the university, policy goals in system steering and policy approaches in system reform. Variation in policymaking persists and might even have become more pronounced. The English case certainly stands out not only in comparison to continental Europe but also within the UK where the Scottish government, for example, has followed different trajectories. In England, waves of reform have followed the idea of higher education as a market and of the university as a service enterprise embedded in this market. Welfare state traditions have by and large been abandoned partly motivated by an ideological stance of the 'marketeers' in English policymaking. In England, 'higher education as a market' is a political project engineered by the state. In contrast, Norway has maintained a strong embeddedness of higher education within the welfare state, offering comparatively generous governmental funding while searching for system efficiency through consultation and incentivizing institutional mergers. Such mergers are also meant to overcome regional disparities in the provision of higher education across the country. In Germany, the legalistic tradition of steering higher education has been supplemented by the discovery of 'the power of the purse' channelling resources in higher education out of basic funding into competitive funding programmes for research and selected universities to compete in the competition for world-class status. In France and Italy, new legislations and other state-directed reforms have been moving public higher education and research substantially away from the Napoleonic tradition of a systemic separation between higher education institutions and separate public research organizations. A modernized version of the Humboldtian idea of the integration of teaching and research within the university is thought to enhance system efficiency and international competitiveness. In Portugal, state reforms aimed at changing state-university relationships towards a supervisory model as well as strengthening the role of research in universities. Governmental interference in university affairs has, however, continued and research tends to be placed into larger interuniversity institutes, pointing at a possible revival of the Napoleonic approach of separating teaching and research. Hungary reminds us of the recent return of populist and nationalistic state interventions into higher education trying to force higher education to line up with the ideological stance of the government.

Our study finds thus quite different paths to system reform activity across Europe illustrating that the governance problem at the systemic level has been addressed in a variety of different ways, according to the specific national context in question and embracing different ideas and roles of the university within this context. There are good reasons to be cautious in assuming a uniform trend in public policies and their impact on organizational configurations across Europe. Templates for the 'modernization' of higher education hit nation states with their own ideational traditions, politico-administrative systems and reform styles that shape the space for political reform. The political adoption of reform templates is likely to be affected by these factors as well as by specific ideas and traditions in the field of higher education. Another note of caution can be drawn from the widespread observation that the relationship between policy intentions and policy outcomes is not linear (Bleiklie, Enders and Lepori 2017). The implementation of 'modernization' agendas interacts with institutional structures and power constellations that cause variations and deviations on the pathway from policy intention to policy outcomes.

The rise of the university as an organization

An important consequence of the changing role of the state in governing higher education has been changing expectations and roles for the university as an organization. In continental Europe, such changes have usually been discursively framed under the banner of university autonomy, relaxing the grip of the state on universities as part and parcel of the politico-administrative state system. In the UK, with its stronger tradition of university autonomy, the political rhetoric has been much more around organizational capabilities for survival and success of universities within competitive quasi-markets. In both cases, however, attention to the university as a 'corporate actor' has increasingly gained importance in the processes of exercising collective coordination. As a consequence of the reshuffling of authority and responsibilities across the different levels in the governance of higher education, the university as an organization has become an important focus of attention in system coordination. Ironically, the idea of the university as a cultural institution vested with values and beliefs that provide legitimacy and support has been in decline, while the idea of the university as an organization has gained in importance.

Devolving authorities to the organizational level form an integral part of New Public Management approaches that stimulated higher education reform across Europe. In this context, the limitations of the state to command and control public sectors and the advantages of devolving authority to local 'corporate actors' are stressed. Universities are thus supposed to act as social entities that possess a certain degree of independence and sovereignty, with partly autonomous and self-interested goals as well as with rational means, commanding independent resources and visible boundaries. As corporate actors, they can make statements and develop and implement strategic actions (De Boer, Enders and Leisyte 2007). Since they can choose and control (part of) their own action, they also become responsible for them. This makes the concept of 'organization' interesting for policymakers and reformers, who are in search of new procedural arrangements to govern a public service sector such as higher education that is growing in size and complexity. From such a perspective it may be wise to share responsibility – as well as problems – with others, that is, with the organizations and their management. At the same time, states' expectations as regards priorities and performances find an addressee in the university as an organization that fits this purpose better than the traditional model of the university characterized by a high degree of internal fragmentation and academic 'multi-vocalism'. The emerging prominence of evaluations and audits also supports this argument. More formal and open accounts and justifications have to be made to the variety of bodies, which claim the right to judge the performance of institutions and their professionals.

A related, though different, factor that supported the rise of the organization concept in higher education is due to the idea of introducing market-like mechanisms and conditions to the sector. Markets need actors, individuals and organizations, that can buy and sell, produce and consume. At the organizational level, universities have in the past not been perceived as producers competing for customers. Scholarly competition for resources and reputation was the 'name of the game', while substantial state-funded growth in higher education dampened any need for further organizational competition among universities. Models such as the service university or the entrepreneurial university signal changes in the beliefs about the role of the university in the marketplace. This goes along with the rise of the customer concept in higher education and the commodification of teaching and research. In this context, the transformation of the university into a 'corporate actor' is thought of as a necessity in order to stimulate market mechanisms.

The 'upgrading' of the university to a 'corporate actor' suggests, however, that the university is transforming from a 'loosely coupled' to a more 'tightly coupled' system. In turn, this has triggered governmental reforms as regards the internal governance of higher education institutions. Through stronger executive leadership and professionalized management structures, strategic capacities of the university as an organization should be strengthened. Another key element of the reforms is to increase the level of competition between universities, to allocate resources according to the performance of the organization as a whole and to shift the focus of state control from procedural matters to output-related monitoring of performance (accountability).

While the idea of strengthening the university as an organizational actor certainly has an appeal to policy-actors, it is not without tensions and dilemmas for which our research provides a rich empirical picture. First, and as we have shown earlier, the state has not disappeared but rather increased its influence that bears on the decision-making within universities depending on contexts and conditions. Classical politico-administrative interference still forms a reality for quite some providers in Europe. Such interference may be due to formal regulatory systems that call for organizational compliance limiting the space of manoeuvre for the university. The state and its bureaucracy may also informally interfere in organizational affairs, even trying to micro-manage them. Further, financial resource dependencies will unavoidably impact on organizational choices. Obviously, this will be the case when institutions heavily rely on governmental funding while being constrained in their capacities to generate other income. Universities and other providers may be allowed to decide internally on the use of governmental funding, while this funding may be bound to performance expectations that cannot be neglected and 'free money' is hard to come by. Universities are also well advised to reconsider their priorities when governments decide to change the funding model. It does, for example, not need a law or decree to incentivize universities in Germany to compete for research grants when the government shifted more and more money into competitive research funding. In England, it did not need a governmental directive demanding the management of student recruitment and a pro-active approach in recruitment on international student markets when governmental funding was mostly replaced by tuition fees. Financial dependencies tend to generate their own directives for organizational behaviour.

Second, we find many examples of the tensions and dilemmas that a supposedly empowered leadership and management is facing within the organization. Across countries, we see reforms towards the 'modernization' of the internal governance of universities taking place which seem to follow certain well-known standard templates: the establishment of university boards which include external stakeholders supposed to represent societal interest within the organization, and providing direction and oversight for the further development of the institution; reforms that give rectors and their leadership teams more managerial and strategic powers in running the organization; a 'modernization' and extension of the management of the university's operational affairs for example in finance, human resources, real estate; and, last but not least, attempts at reducing the internal powers of the academic estate within the organization. However, we see a patchwork of different regulatory systems emerging across Europe instead of a unified pattern (see Chapter 3). Boards may include external stakeholders only or may be composed of external members and internal academic members. Their role may be confined to the control of operational affairs or to the development of strategic directions of the organization, or a mix of both. Rectors and deans may be appointed eliminating part of their traditional dependency on the academic estate or they may still be elected following the more traditional patterns of leadership selection. Senates may have been abolished or may have become rather neglected discussion fora; they may need to be consulted or may need to be formally assigned to decide on leadership plans for organizational change. In some countries, universities have some choice among different options of how to structure their internal governance and to shape their internal power relations. In sum, we find considerable variation among countries as regards the form and extent of political changes within the structure of the internal university governance. Across countries, we observe that different types of institutions provide another source of variation for internal governance structures and practices. By and large, more research-intensive universities tend to be 'less managerial' than their more teaching-intensive counterparts. The status and reputation of the research university provides a certain buffer against governmental intervention for governance reform, respect for some involvement of academics in decision-making is more deeply written into their institutional culture, and leaders and managers will be more aware of the organizations' dependence on the reputation and funding that academics bring to them.

Certainly, the perception that 'the academics are a problem' for the corporate actorhood of the university has been part and parcel of reforms that not only strengthened leadership and management but also weakened the formal powers of the academic estate. Chapter 3 highlights how such reform attempts have met different traditions in university governance where the continental European model provided levels of faculty independence and devolved powers not to be found in the Anglophone model. In addition to political pressures, such different traditions may help to understand why the idea of the university managed from the top has found its strongest expression in the UK. Somehow academics seem, however, to tend to get in the way. There may be formal internal regulations that demand the consultation of academics if not co-decision-making with academic senates, departments and deans. Top-down command and control is not really an option when compliance with such formal requirements is demanded. Informal communication channels may persist with important mechanisms linking management and the academic heartland providing input into organizational decision-making and paving the way for the implementation of organizational changes. When such formal and informal channels break down and a managerialist approach takes over, the university is in danger of becoming a house divided against itself or a machine bureaucracy that drives efficiency while losing capacity for creativity and innovation (Shattock and Horvath 2019).

Finally, the idea of the university as a corporate actor is a fascinating while curious one given that it assumes that the organization can be treated as a single entity where the highest levels of authority can exercise similar powers as to those operating in business. This idea of the university as a single actor has been reinforced by governmental reforms, evaluations, rankings and funding schemes that take the organization as a whole as their focal point and consider interorganizational competition as the most important form of competition in the field. Often drawing on organizational models from the private corporate sector, much of the rhetoric behind the idea of the university as a single corporate organization has suggested that they should become more similar to companies competing in product, capital and labour markets, and entrepreneurial activities. As we have seen governmental reforms have not always lived up to their own rhetoric, providing procedural autonomy rather than substantive autonomy under the condition that universities align to governmental expectations and priorities. There are also good reasons to question the idea of the university as a unified actor looking at its internal fragmentation and external embeddedness in manifold academic tribes and territories. Universities are agglomerations of a variety of academic fields and subfields that do not necessarily share the same characteristics. Their intellectual culture and communication styles are different; their links to fields of practice in teaching and research, and to external stakeholders, are different; they are embedded in different disciplinary funding environments; they may be strong in attracting students while not as strong in performing in the research market, and vice versa. In addition, reputation and funding rely to a considerable extent on the judgement of their peers outside the university. Under such conditions, leadership and management can be expected to be involved in a constant struggle to establish some unity within diversity. Even where states did delegate substantial operational autonomy to university managers and enhance their internal powers relative to the academic professionals, this will not inevitably lead to their effective control of research and teaching activities such that they can realistically be held responsible for each universities' success or failure in achieving agreed objectives. Under such conditions strategic independence need not 'imply effective managerial determination of who carries out which activities in what ways that collectively contribute to overall organisational purposes' (Whitley and Gläser 2014, p. 44).

The integration and differentiation of the higher education landscape

Both the expansion of higher education and its 'modernization' have led to continuous efforts to balance unity and diversity, system integration and differentiation in higher education. In talking, for instance, about 'elite' and 'mass' higher education, 'diversification and stratification', 'binary systems', 'non-university' higher education or the 'research university' the understanding and reform of the institutional landscape within a national system of higher education have become important issues. Since the 1960s, public debate and policy reform have been concerned with the institutional configuration of higher education across national systems in Europe. In this context, the national scale was already supplemented by the idea of the 'regional university' as a sub-level within the national field. Over recent decades, the European dimension gained in importance adding an international scale to the dynamics around the unity and diversity of the higher education landscape. The emergence of global rankings and of discourses on the global organizational archetype of the 'world-class university' finally embedded the idea of the university on a global scale.

Chapter 3 discusses how Germany, the UK and France were the first to experience demographic pressures of social demand for higher education and economic pressures to link higher education more closely to the needs of national and regional labour markets. Each country found its own way of expanding the field while the common pattern had been expanding existing institutions, creating new ones and most importantly creating and expanding a new tier of 'non-university' institutions with a more teaching-oriented role, more vocational curricula, often more specialized in their subject base and more regionally oriented. This pattern was also adopted in Hungary, Norway and Portugal. In consequence, higher education became a much broader church including institutions that would traditionally not have been considered a university proper. In countries with a strong Humboldtian tradition, the honorary title of university has in fact still not been granted to the new type of institutions (Germany) or depends on their capacity to show a visible involvement in research and doctoral training (Norway). In every country the boundaries between such tiers have, however, become more blurred, and in some countries the divides between university and non-university sectors have even been abolished. In those where they have been maintained, they are reportedly under pressure, especially due to the pressures associated with 'mission drift', rising aspirations of lower-tier institutions to gain in status and recognition and attempts of 'research universities' to integrate more vocationally oriented programmes into the offerings. This has often been a motivation for introducing additional changes in the systemic and institutional governance of higher education where states followed, however, different trajectories depending on the size of the field, the degree of politically incentivized concentration of research funding within the field and policies for the regional engagement of higher education institutions.

Our research thus points also to the relevance of the 'regional' scale for the unity and diversity of the field. This comes in two different shapes: the politico-administrative structure of the state itself and the mobilization of higher education for regional development within the country. In a federal state like Germany, a considerable political responsibility for higher education rests in the hands of the Länder. This might be expected to be a potential source of intra-country differentiation that is, however, kept within quite limited bounds because the country's constitution demands equal living conditions and public service provisions across the country, and because the states have confined themselves to joined-up decision-making in educational affairs. In a unitary country, the UK, the devolution of political authority to the four home nations might in fact have led to a somewhat more differentiated political landscape than we find in Germany. In addition, the political organization of the higher education field itself in self-selected groupings, called university mission groups, follows the logic of stratification in UK higher education and undermines attempts of different types of universities to speak with one voice.

Further, our study points at the renaissance of the idea of the regional role of the university and related policies. Again, political discourses and reform styles across Europe differ markedly ranging from motivations for the regional university based on social inclusiveness to motivations based on economic prosperity, from bottom-up approaches to top-down approaches for policy implementation. It is clear though that regional consideration plays an important role for the political design of the field, and for the unity and diversity of the field. In many countries, higher education institutions have, of course, always had some role in their region just by being there. They contribute to the socio-economic standing and development of the region, for example, due to investments into their infrastructure, the private spending of their staff and students, and their decision to keep students and graduates within the region or attract students from other parts of the country to the region. In addition, universities, their staff and students also contribute to the cultural and political life of the region. Such positive impacts of higher education on regional development and the effect of such linkages on regional employment and income are well known and continue to be important. In the process of expansion, states have thus used the establishment of new institutions as a tool to support structurally weaker regions. This does not, however, necessarily imply that such institutions include the regional outreach into their role and mission, and regional outreach may not receive special attention and institution-wide support in the governance of the institution. In contrast, the regionally engaged university perceives itself as a central actor in the regional development. It aims at actively influencing regional development as a change agent. Its governance addresses regional development with a view on the overall profile, resources and competences of the institution.

Recently, institutional unity and diversity are also embedded internationally and changes in the regulatory system across Europe have been attributed a growing influence in the debate on the European university. Arguably, the rise of the European Higher Education Area and that of the European Research Area show that European-level debates and policymaking processes have been paying growing attention to the European university as well as to the issue of the unity and diversity of the European higher education landscape. In this respect, multi-level policies aimed at the European university provide an interesting case. In Europe, universities have played an important role in the making of modern nation states including the building of a national heritage and identity, the formation and reproduction of national elites, the preparation and selection of the governmental and administrative workforce, and the provision of research for national economic and social development. Traditionally, higher education and research were thus supposed to be national affairs, making it difficult to institutionalize European-level responsibilities and policies for this area even though respective initiatives can be traced back to the 1950s. It is in the 1990s that the issue of the unity and diversity of the European higher education system gained in dynamic and is embedded in new ways intergovernmentally and supranationally.

The rise of the European Higher Education Area and that of the European Research Area have added another international layer to the struggle about an appropriate institutional design for the European university. Both developments are not neutral to the issue of systemic differentiation.

The European Higher Education Area revolves around concepts such as 'harmonization', 'convergence' and 'coordination', while the European Research Area stresses concepts such as 'excellence', 'relevance', 'critical mass' and 'stratification' (Enders and De Boer 2009). The map of the landscape as regards the teaching function and the research function of higher education thus seems to become increasingly dissociated.

Arguably, the university has also been increasingly included in processes of globalization. International organizations, such as the OECD, UNESCO and the World Bank, have become visible political players in the field. International student mobility experienced substantial growth. Countries and institutions alike have become more proactive in recruiting in the international student 'market' driven by financial and reputational considerations. The global map of countries figuring prominently in knowledge production in the world of science has also become more colourful. Within this context, the pursuit of the idea of the 'world-class' university has been spreading across the globe. Internationally, nationally and organizationally, excellence in international higher education has become a matter of policy that affects diverse interests. Global rankings form an important input and stimulation in this positional competition for 'world-class' status in times of global educational expansion and global interconnectedness of higher education (Hazelkorn 2015).

Such rankings construct their object of comparison – the 'world-class' university – introducing the idea that potentially all universities around the world can be measured and ranked according to the same standards. Differences in context, conditions and missions of institutions disappear, leading to the de-contextualization of universities within the rankings. This allows rankings to produce a hierarchy of institutions within a simple and clear rank order. Differences between institutions do not matter except that they can be expressed as a matter of better or worse within a pre-defined space of performance. Rankings produce what they measure: an imagined 'world-class' university that can be calculated according to standardized norms of excellence.

Such global comparisons are made in relation to one model of the university: the comprehensive research-intensive university. This university model, most prominently developed in the leading American research universities, lends itself to the formation of a single global competition constructed in the rankings that build on established notions of what constitutes a 'world-class' university. It is thus not surprising that American universities are holding leading positions in these rankings. They stimulate investment according to the rules of the ranking game as universities as well as countries to strive to improve their competitive positions (Enders 2014). The growing number of institutions and countries engaging with the idea of 'world class' seems to suggest processes of organizational isomorphism and policy convergence that need, however, to be treated with care. While discourses might be dominated by the 'world-class' university as the apex of the global field, most of the institutions in our study see their role as a national or regional player. If they engage with rankings, it will be national league tables providing visibility and distinction within the country. Smaller countries may not be able or willing to invest into the global ranking game, prioritizing their national goals for the 'modernization' of higher education. The UK had introduced a national research evaluation exercise aiming at concentrating research funding long before global rankings appeared and seems to be relying on the visibility of its traditional elite universities in global rankings. In contrast, Germany and France have invested selected research funding into 'excellence', reshaping the national field by concentrating research funding; aligning research universities and public research organizations outside higher education more closely; and, in the case of France, merging the *grandes ecoles* into the political project. The global academic arms race is not for everyone and might play out in different ways.

The 'modernization' of higher education revisited

Attempts to delineate some common elements of the multiple transformations of the university point to the unfolding of a most interesting paradox. The European university is undeniably a success story. Research and teaching have expanded enormously; the fields of research and scholarship have multiplied and provide potential links to all other subsystems in modern society. There are not only no signs of stagnation but expectations as regards the contribution of higher education and research to the 'European knowledge society' are growing. Modern societies and their subsystems all seek new innovations and expect the universities to deliver these goods. In parallel with success, criticism of the European university has been coming more and more to the fore – on the national level as well as on the European level. There is concern about the responsiveness of the university to socio-economic demands as well as its incapacities of organizational self-steering in an increasingly competitive environment. In sum, the changing nature and role of knowledge for society seems to be accompanied by changes in university-society relationships that are a mixed blessing for the status and role of higher education.

One way of getting a better understanding of the institutional dynamics of the university is to look at mission overload. The term 'mission overload' addresses a situation in which ever-growing and (partly) contradictory demands and expectations are put on the institution at stake. In higher education, mission overload certainly has a quantitative component due to the expansion of the field in education and the substantial growth in research. It also has a qualitative component due to growing number of demands to contribute to solving socio-economic problems of the 'knowledge society'. Finally, there is a procedural component as regards more efficient means of goal achievement in higher education as a multi-purpose and multi-product institution serving ever more stakeholders. Such developments are external as well as internal to the university. They stimulate reforms that challenge traditional ideas of the university and its institutional form.

Our study reveals convergence as well as divergence across Europe as regards the role of the state *vis-à-vis* higher education, the organizational form and governance of higher education institutions, and the unity and diversity of the higher education landscape. Everywhere states have become more active in trying to rationalize and 'modernize' the field according to governmental priorities. Within this context, the idea of the university as an institution, in the sense of a societal sub-system vested with beliefs and values that provide legitimacy and secure financial support, has been in decline. A more utilitarian idea of the university contributing to national competitiveness and economic growth has gained in importance. Following Max Weber (>1917<, 1968), we might say that we observe a process of demystification (*Entzauberung*) of the idea of the university. Countries traditionally characterized by a strong welfare state tradition have maintained some elements of the idea of the university as a cultural institution while it has most clearly disappeared when the neoliberal state works as a market engineer. International templates for reform, such as New Public Management, have travelled across countries, importantly though with different timing and influence. Profound differences can still be found among European countries in what their political priorities for higher education are, how they frame their political goals, and how they implement their policies. Variation in policymaking persists and might even have become more pronounced reflecting different ideational traditions, political-administrative structures, and domain specific ideas and beliefs that appear in the field of higher education.

A similar statement might be made about the emergence of the university as a more important 'corporate actor' in the governance of the system. The decline of the university as an institution has been accompanied by the rise of the university as an organization. Attempts at aligning the university as a public agency more closely with the political priorities of the state, and the state-engineered transformation of the university into a service enterprise in the marketplace have both been accompanied by calls to strengthen the organizational actorhood of the university. Across countries, we see reforms towards the 'modernization' of the internal governance of universities seemingly following a well-known standard template: the establishment of university boards; reforms that give rectors and their leadership team more managerial and strategic powers; a 'modernization' and extension of the management of the university's operational affairs; attempts at reducing the internal powers of the academic estate within the organization. However, below this surface, we see a patchwork of different rule systems emerging across Europe instead of a unified pattern of 'modernization'. States and their higher education institutions were often not willing or not capable of pushing for a wholesale turn of the university into a 'corporate actor'. This has led to hybrid forms of the university as a managed professional organization; a model that comes in different shapes depending on the national and organizational context, and that is not without tensions and dilemmas for management and academics alike.

Finally, the idea of the university has been profoundly affected by higher education becoming a much broader church including on the one hand institutions that would traditionally not necessarily have been considered a university, and on the other hand institutions being praised as 'world class' universities. We see research and teaching being more and more separated in political priorities and expectations, in the conditional supply of funding, and in the higher education landscape. At the same time, the idea and role of the university is no longer confined to the nation state even though national contexts and conditions still play an important role. The university has also become a regional, a European and a global institution. Daniel Bell (1973) could write about the role of the university in the post-industrial society within a primarily national context while variegated ideas of the university now aim to meet not only national demands but also regional, European and global scales in society and economy. The European university has gone multi-scalar and is embedded in various nested organizational fields: a global field, a European field, national fields and regional fields that shape field dynamics. Historically, higher education governance structures in Europe developed in three main patterns: the Napoleonic, the Humboldtian and the Anglophone, whose legacy certainly had an impact on how the 'modernization' of higher education played out. All of them have, however, come under substantial institutional pressure to change.

6

Convergence and Divergence in the Developing Governance of European Higher Education

There is little doubt that the combined effects of massification and austerity have encouraged a common search for system management solutions. The state has become more dominant; accountability mechanisms, financial and academic, have grown in importance. In addition, the Bologna Process has been a catalyst for modernization particularly in countries like Hungary and Portugal, where reform had been held back by political change. In all the continental European systems higher education continued to be funded directly from the public purse, with only Scotland of the UK nations following suit; England represented a clear outlier in introducing a tuition fee-funded system and adopting aggressive market principles as the basis for managing the system. Wales also challenged the pattern, but from a different policy perspective, by adopting a tertiary education system which offered a more articulated approach than higher education systems elsewhere. Even with these two exceptions it is possible to argue that there was a considerable degree of convergence amongst European states in addressing the problems arising from increasing numbers, rising costs and the need for governance reform.

But against this must be weighed further political divergence: the fact of the UK's leaving the European Union and the clear rejection of a directly publicly funded system of higher education in England by the governing political party; and in Hungary the expulsion of the Central European University and the imposition of direct managerial control through chancellors appointed by the government and by small governing bodies also appointed by government and freighted by political appointees. Equally one might draw a distinction between the government regimes of Northern

Europe (Germany, the Netherlands and the Scandinavian states) and those of middle and southern Europe. Here, while the formulae and language of reform may be similar, the implementation and political processes involved are very different. Convergence and divergence may thus be said to be occurring simultaneously: the superficial descriptions of the establishment of new approaches to system management may overlay profound differences in political and social character which serve to drive higher education systems in very different directions. While at one level European states appear to be following a broadly common pattern in managing the 'modernization' of their higher education systems, below the surface individual contexts, cultural and geopolitical characteristics, academic traditions and access to financial support provide a more differentiated picture.

We have found that the concept of the state steering at a distance and of universities being empowered to determine their own destiny is considerably at variance with the reality of state – university relationships in Europe at the beginning of the 2020s. The evidence suggests that governments have been much more managerially interventionist in the operation of their higher education systems and, in some cases, in the details of institutional governance, than the proponents of New Public Management theory anticipated. The outcomes, however, have had the effect of creating greater convergence of systems in some respects: the English system, once the clearest example of 'hands-off' state governance, has dispensed with a politically neutral intermediary body and opened up the system to close and direct engagement with a minster, as well as being subject to a state-run regulatory body, thus paralleling the position in most continental systems where governments may have devolved operational management to the universities but retain significant powers of intervention in system management. Where there is divergence, however, is in the way governments arrive at decisions on higher education: in Norway and in Wales the process is infinitely consensual, with frequent consultations and opportunities to comment from inside and outside the system, whereas in England and Hungary one sees little evidence of any search for partnership between the institutions and their representatives and the government of the day. This would not be the case in Germany, where decision-making can be slow between the central organs of government, the Länder governments and the institutions but the process itself encourages stability and trust.

Convergence is reinforced by a general desire to strengthen institutional management, particularly the powers of rectors and vice chancellors, although their designation as 'chief executive' remains a step too far for continental universities. But universities in all systems have come increasingly to devolve management functions to executive teams and continental universities seem to be moving slowly towards following UK and US practice by replacing electoral processes within institutions with appointed processes aimed at attracting academic leaders and managers from outside. At the level of pro-rectors, pro-vice chancellors and deans, however, this universally distances the academic community from governance in their own institution with a complementary loss of trust and commitment. While there is a wide variety in the constitutional and internal political powers of rectors and their executive teams between the different university systems, the trend towards strengthening their authority in operational and strategic issues represents a common realignment in all countries.

An important element in this realignment is reflected in the admission of external (lay) members into institutional governance, something that had previously been unknown in continental universities but which was traditional in the UK except in Oxford and Cambridge. The main reforming influence here were the boards of regents or trustees in US universities where, as in the UK, the key historical concept of lay involvement in university governance was not control but machinery to achieve some element of external democratic involvement in the affairs of public institutions. This was exemplified in a US definition of a board of regents as 'The moat and the bridge' to the community (Epstein 1974). The introduction of US-style boards was recommended by Aghion *et al.* (2010) essentially on managerial and strategic grounds and strongly urged by the EU Commission but attracted little initial enthusiasm in continental Europe where it was opposed by academic communities resistant to the implied loss of institutional and academic autonomy. The result was a lukewarm acceptance of the presence of lay members on governing boards but resistance to allowing them a majority. In Germany, for example, where some Länder preserved a lay majority, key strategic decision-making remained with the senate. By contrast, in the UK the pressure was all the other way, with lay majority boards that had previously worked in close partnership with senates being encouraged by government over time to act more like company boards where the state, through its Office for Students, served as the proxy shareholder. Thus while it can be said that there is convergence on the principle of the introduction of external lay members into institutional governance, there is little convergence in practice: there are considerable variations within continental countries, with Hungary at one end of the spectrum and Norway at the other, and in the UK, where the authority of academic boards *vis-à-vis* their governing bodies in teaching-intensive institutions differs significantly from that exercised by senates in research-intensive universities, even where it has been reduced, and where the two oldest universities, Oxford and Cambridge, have been able to resist all pressures to include lay voices in their structures.

Divergence also applies in the question of academic staff participation in governance. It is clear that in Germany and in research-intensive universities in the UK strong senates continue to play an important role in institutional governance but senates do not exist at all in Norway, and in other countries (and in the UK) their role can be reduced to rubber-stamping decisions that emanate from the rectorate or the faculties. A significant division exists between the Anglophone and the continental countries' powers vested in faculties. In the UK, faculty boards are representative of departments and report to senates/academic boards, but except perhaps in the case of medical schools, they are not necessarily powerful in their own interests in strategic or key management decision-making. The authority of the vice chancellor and the executive will outweigh special faculty pleading. In continental Europe, however, the faculty powerbase remains strong, and Chapter 3 provides examples where rectors' and senates' powers are clearly circumscribed by faculties and where deans and deans' committee can seriously restrict rectorial decision-making. These are powers which hardly exist in the UK, where academic staff are increasingly pushed to the periphery in decision-making by the increased authority of centralized management machinery. In a continental university one might argue that there are too many potential roadblocks to decisive decision-making, while in the UK there are often not enough. Although it is difficult to generalize, it can be said that the academic communities in continental universities are able in present conditions to exercise greater control over institutional policy issues than would be the case in the UK in spite of the efforts by the EU and individual governments to 'modernize' the systems.

At the same time there is no evidence to suggest that academics suffer restrictions in what they teach and in creating or revising courses, although in Hungary and Portugal external agencies can impose severe limitations on their institutions' ability to proceed. Both represent severe constraints on institutional academic autonomy. Moreover in Hungary the imposition of the Chancellor system giving powers to a non-academic to intervene at department, faculty and senate level on matters of financial viability (Chapter 3) represents an ultimate example of state intervention to limit academic autonomy.

A somewhat surprising area of convergence is the role of the student body in institutional governance. From a period of great turbulence in the past, what we found, as explained in Chapter 4, was a stable regime of internal representation across all the countries we interviewed in. Student officials made it clear that they were heavily engaged with curriculum review, in proposals in respect to new courses and teaching quality, that they had regular meetings with senior university officials and had representation on senates and governing boards. The level of representation and the powers that went with it could vary but the principle of representation was unquestioned, even when their voting strength on senate could determine a contested issue. What was remarkable was how unremarkable the student engagement with governance actually was and how unremarkable were the issues that it addressed – in practice much more domestic than policy oriented. Representation at a national level was more mixed and seemed to fluctuate to reflect particular issues rather than to have a measured impact on policy.

In other respects divergence is considerably more apparent. The first of these reflects the steps that countries took to meet geopolitical challenges and the pressures of massification. Thus policies in Hungary, Norway and Portugal had to address the 'hinterland' issue where higher education was required to decentralise itself from the hold of the traditional centres of learning in historically prosperous urban locations. In the case of two countries, Germany and Norway, policy was also driven by a formal determination to ensure equality of provision across regions. In parallel, the effects of massification were to lead all countries to the need to create new university institutions or upgrade existing institutions to match the demands of student number expansion. These pressures were transformative of the existing national higher education systems, and the resolution of the emerging 'binary lines' between the historic university systems and the new, reflected the differing characteristics of each national system. Germany chose to reinforce its university system and preserve a sharp distinction between the universities and the Fachhochschulen; the UK created a unified system by upgrading the polytechnics *en bloc*; other countries imposed provisions or regulations to distinguish between institutions and introduced the title of 'university of applied science' to recognize ambiguities.

A significant component of these decisions was the place of research. Thus in Norway and Scotland full university titles depended on the institutions being designated as research-active and in Germany the segmentation of the university and the Fachhochschulen was entirely research determined. By contrast in England the concept of the 'teaching only' university was widely shared among policymakers. A further significant related divergence was the introduction of institutional (or disciplinary) research evaluation. First incorporated into system management as early as 1985–6 in the UK, it has been primarily responsible for the creation of a steep university hierarchy which to a considerable extent mirrors institutional performance above and below the previous binary line. Germany, France and Italy have followed the process although in a less draconian manner than in the UK but the overall, and intended, effect that is being produced is to increase institutional differentiation within systems. Chapter 5 describes how the idea of the university in Europe is being extended but the extensions are different country to country and may therefore be said to accelerate divergence.

A further divergence can be seen in the national level of management of research policy with both Germany and the UK separating Ministerial responsibility for research from responsibilities for higher education thus potentially undermining the traditional concept of the integration of research and teaching in universities. The organizational dangers of this separation can perhaps be seen in practice in Portugal, where for the laudable reasons of providing research opportunities to academics in new, second-tier, institutions and improving universities' chances of winning EU Horizon funding for research projects, joint university disciplinary-based research centres have been founded on sites separate from the main university campuses. This has the benefit of maximizing research expertise but also has the effect of isolating research and researchers from main university activities and denuding main campuses of a climate of research. Administratively these centres are inevitably developing independently of the institutions that founded them in a manner that could profoundly change the system and undo the considerable modernizing reform effort which has been undertaken together by the state and the universities in the last thirty years. It must be hoped that ways may be found to prevent a divorce occurring.

But perhaps the major driver of divergence is the funding agenda and the different performativity targets which may accompany it. Massification has put inordinate strains on public finance and in the UK has resulted in the growing marketization of the system by a substitution of student-paid tuition fees for government recurrent funding except in Scotland where a fee-paid approach has always been resisted. No European state has followed. Perhaps as significant is that in England the state controls the fee levels charged to home students and can vary them to put pressure on the system. (A by-product of the UK's departure from the EU is that student numbers from the other European countries have fallen sharply because they are being charged as if they were international students.) One result is that English, Welsh and Northern Irish universities have tended to become more 'commercially' led in their culture and decision-making although the language of consumerism is by no means absent from continental universities perhaps under the influence of performativity targets. However, the fact that in all the continental countries we studied the state covered between 80 per cent and 90 per cent of their institutions' budget had a considerable impact on state-university relationships. One might have thought that the creation of a market in the UK (except in Scotland) would have provided institutions with greater freedom but in practice interventions by the state have increased and its retention of the power to regulate fee levels have given it a leverage no less than that enjoyed by states which are the majority funding agency. But within the latter category the differences of funding levels, performance targets and of the funding balances between research and teaching monies emphasise that national ambitions and changes in student demography will combine to create increasingly diverse systems.

Indeed what becomes evident is that divergence is driven chiefly by nation states, not by the institutions. Partly this is the result of differing geophysical characteristics and the outturns of individual national economies, partly the result of political positions that have been adopted, partly the absence of predetermined commitments to equality across regions but however construed what we found was that the more the state has become interventionist the greater the divergence within European higher education has occurred. While the Bologna Process drew European higher education together systemic reforms have cumulatively encouraged a greater drawing apart.

In 2010 when the European Higher Education Area was established the expectation built on the success of the Bologna Process was for a convergence of European higher education and the adoption of reforms in higher education on the basis of common key values. Our evidence suggests that rather than greater convergence the interim period has seen greater divergence in governance structures and in the exercise of national policies. The wave of enthusiasm for modernization on 'European' lines unleashed by the Lisbon Declaration has run its course, and countries are reverting to national solutions aimed at what they deem to be national issues. The future is likely to see an increasing differentiation in European higher education.

References

Chapter 1
(1) P.1.5.3
(2) G.1.1.19
(3) H.2.7.3
(4) N.1.3.4
(5) N.2.3.11
(6) P.1.1.6
(7) P.1.1.8
(8) H.1.3.10
(9) H.2.8.9–10
(10) H.2.9.21
(11) G.2.5.4
(12) G.1.2.7
(13) G.2.1.3
(14) G3.5.18
(15) G.3.1.7
(16) G.1.2.6
(17) G.3.2.5
(18) G.3.2.2
(19) G.1.2.12
(20) N.1.9.4
(21) N.2.1.3
(22) N.1.1.13
(23) N.2.1.5
(24) N.2.1.11
(25) W.A.13.7
(26) W.A.13.7
(27) W.1.1.1
(28) H.3.7.15
(29) H.5.1.2
(30) H.2.7.10
(31) H.2.9.21
(32) H.3.2.7
(33) H.1.1.11
(34) H.1.1
(35) P.1.8.2
(36) P.1.10.5
(37) P.1.5.5
(38) P.1.10.3
(39) P.1.5.3
(40) P.1.5.4
(41) P.2.4.6
(42) G.1.1.11
(43) G.1.1.5
(44) P.1.1.3
(45) P.1.5.6
(46) P.3.2.10
(47) P.1.3.12
(48) H.2.3.3–4
(49) H.2.7.16
(50) N.2.3.11

Chapter 2
(1) H.1.1.6
(2) P.2.3.10–11
(3) P.3.1.1–4
(4) P.1.5.14
(5) P.3.1.6
(6) P.2.8.2
(7) P.3.1.6
(8) P.2.2.1
(9) P.2.1.4
(10) P.3.2.7–8
(11) H.3.4.7
(12) H.1.4.13
(13) H.3.3.12

(14) N.3.6.11
(15) N.2.3.5
(16) N.1.9.5
(17) N.2.1.8–9
(18) H.3.3.11
(19) H.4.1.4
(20) P.2.8.2
(21) N.3.5.9
(22) H.1.2.2
(23) H.1.2.3
(24) H.1.5.4
(25) N.1.2.3

Chapter 3
(1) G.2.4.1
(2) G.2.5.1
(3) G.2.7.3
(4) G.2.4.6
(5) G.2.4.2
(6) G.3.1.3
(7) G.1.2.8
(8) G.2.3.10
(9) G.2.3.10
(10) G.2.7.6
(11) N.1.2.9
(12) N.1.9.5
(13) N.1.7.5
(14) N.1.10.7
(15) N.3.1.13
(16) N.3.1.12
(17) N.1.3.1
(18) N.1.10.16
(19) N.1.3.7
(20) H.2.2.17
(21) H.3.4.1
(22) H.2.9.21
(23) H.1.1.8–9
(24) H.1.4.11
(25) H.3.7.15

(26) H.2.7.15
(27) H.3.1.2
(28) H.2.7.8
(29) H.2.2.6
(30) H.2.7.15
(31) H.2.8.6
(32) H.2.6.11
(33) H.3.3.2
(34) H.3.5.13
(35) H.2.4.12
(36) H.2.3.2
(37) H.2.6.3–4
(38) H.1.6.17
(39) P.1.2.5
(40) P.2.2.5
(41) P.1.5.3
(42) P.1.3.17
(43) P.1.3.15
(44) P.1.1.14
(45) P.1.10.17
(46) P.1.10.18
(47) H.3.3.14

Chapter 4
(1) A.2.20
(2) N.3.8.3.5
(3) G.2.2.3–4
(4) N.1.8.2
(5) P.1.4.6
(6) G.2.2.1
(7) E.1.6.8
(8) H.2.4.18
(9) A.2.17
(10) A.2.17
(11) P.1.4.4–5
(12) E.1.6.12–13
(13) G.2.2.8–9
(14) E.4.6.16
(15) N.1.8.13

References

(16) H.2.4.4–5
(17) N.1.8.8
(18) H.2.4.4
(19) E.1.6.2
(20) N.1.8.12
(21) E.4.6.4
(22) P.1.4.4–5
(23) H.2.4.14
(24) N.1.8.13
(25) P.2.7.6
(26) N.3.8.4
(27) N.1.8.16–17
(28) P.1.4.9
(29) P.2.7.4
(30) G.3.3.7
(31) E.3.6.11
(32) E.4.6.13
(33) N.1.8.19
(34) H.3.5.14
(35) P.1.4.6–7
(36) P.2.7.1–2
(37) N.3.8.1
(38) N.3.7.6–7
(39) H.2.4.9
(40) S.2.7.12–13
(41) E.5.7.10–11
(42) P.1.4.2

(43) H.2.7.1–2
(44) N.1.5.3
(45) N.3.9.5–8
(46) P.1.3.4–5
(47) G.2.3.7
(48) N.1.9.10–11
(49) N.3.11.10.12
(50) P.1.10.1
(51) E.2.4.16–17
(52) P.1.1.1
(53) N.1.5.5
(54) P.1.1.12–13
(55) P.1.8 2–3
(56) H.1.3.5–7
(57) H.3.4.13
(58) N.3.2.2–3
(59) G.2.7.12–13
(60) E.3.5.3.15
(61) E.4.5.12–13
(62) E.5.4.2.4
(63) P.1.1.12–13
(64) P.2.11.5–6
(65) H.2.1.13
(66) H.3.8.13–15
(67) E.3.16–17
(68) N.1.7.10–11
(69) G.2.3.14

Works Cited

Adams, R (2018) 'Universities facing cash shortfalls will not be propped up–regulator'. *The Guardian.* 1 January.

Aghion, P, Dewatripont, M, Hoxley, C, Mas-Colell, A, and Sapir, A (2010) 'The governance and performance of universities: Evidence from Europe and the US'. *Economic Policy* 25, 61.

Bell, D (1973) *The Coming of Post-Industrial Society: A Venture in Social Forecasting.* New York: Basic Books.

Bird, R (1994) 'Reflections on the British Government and higher education in the 1980s'. *Higher Education Quarterly* 48(2).

Blackmore, J, Brennan, M, Zipin, L, and Carrick, M A (2010) 'Repositioning university governance and academic work'. Blackmore, J, Brennan, M and Zipin, L *Educational Futures* 41 Web.

Bleike, I, Enders, J, and Lepori, B (2017) 'Setting the stage theory and research questions'. In Bleike, I, Enders, J, and Lepori, B (Eds.), *Managing Universities, Policy and Organizational Change from a Western European Perspective.* London: Macmillan, 3–30.

Brooks, R, Byford, K, and Sela, K (2015) 'The changing role of students' unions within contemporary higher education'. *Journal of Education Policy* 30(2), 165–81.

Cardoso, A H (1989) A universidade portuguesa e o poder autonómico. Revista Crítica de CiŒncias Sociais, 27/28, 125–145[as cited in Gonçalves, M. E. (2012) 'Changing Legal Regimes and the Fate of Autonomy in Portuguese Universities'. In Neave, G, and Amaral, A (2012) *Higher Education in Portugal 1974–2009: A Nation, a Generation.* Springer Science Business Media B.V., 161–79. Retrieved May 3, 2022, from http://0-dx.doi.org.fama.us.es/10.1007/978-94-007-2135-7.]

Carswell, J (1985) *Government and the Universities.* Cambridge: Cambridge University Press.

Chartelain-Portney, S, Mignot-Gerard, S Musselin, C, and Sporiam, S (2014) 'The impact of recent reforms in the institutional governance of French universities'. In Shattock, M L (Ed.), *International Trends in University Governance.* Abingdon: Routledge, 67–88.

Clark, B R (1983) *The Higher Education System.* Berkeley: University of California Press.

Commission of the European Communities (CEC) (2003) *The Role of Universities in the Europe of Knowledge.* Communication from the Commission COM 2003/58. Brussels: CEC.

Commission of the European Communities (CEC) (2005) *Mobilising the Brain Power of Europe: Enabling Universities to Make Their Full Contribution to the Lisbon Strategy.* Communication from the Commission COM 2005/152. Brussels: CEC.

Commission of the European Communities (CEC) (2006) *Delivering on the Modernization Agenda for Universities: Education, Research and Innovation.* Communication from the Commission COM 2006/208. Brussels: CEC.

Committee on Higher Education (1963) *Higher Education: A Report (the Robbins Report).* London: HMSO Cmnd 2154.

Committee of University Chairs (2020) *Higher Education Code of Governance.* Committee of University Chairs.

Committee of Vice-Chancellors and Principles (1985) *The Report of the Steering Committee on Efficiency Studies in Universities (the Jarratt Report).* London: CVCP.

De Boer, H F, Enders, J, and Leisyte, L (2007) 'Public sector reform in Dutch higher education: The organizational transformation of the university'. *Public Administration* 85(1), 27–46.

De Boer, H and Enders, J (2017) 'Working in the shadow of hierarchy: Organizational autonomy and external influence'. In Bleike, I, Enders, J, and Labori, B (Eds.), *Managing Universities Policy and Organizational Change from a Western European Perspective.* London: Macmillan, 57–83.

De Boer, H, Jongblood, H, Enders, J, and File, J (2009) *Progress in Higher Education Reform in Europe Part 1 Governance Reform.* CHEPS.

Department of Business, Innovation and Skills (2016) *Success as a Knowledge Economy: Teaching Excellence, Social Mobility and Student Choice.* HMSO Cm 5892.

Enders, J (2014) 'The academic arms race: International rankings and global competition for 'World Class Universities''. In Pettigrew, A M, Cornuel, E and Hommel, U (Eds.), *The Institutional Development of Business Schools.* Oxford: Oxford University Press, 155–75.

Enders, J, and De Boer, H F (2009) 'The mission impossible of the European university: Institutional confusion and institutional diversity'. In Amaral, A, Neave, G, Musselin, C and Maassen, P (Eds.), *European Integration and the Governance of Higher Education and Research* (Higher Education Dynamics Vol 26). Dordrecht: Springer, 159–78.

Enders, J, De Boer, H, and Leisyte, L (2009) 'New public management and the academic profession: The rationalization of academic work revisited'. In Enders, J and de Weert, E (Eds.), *The Changing Face of Academic Life: Issues in Higher Education.* London: Palgrave Macmillan, 36–57.

Epstein, L D (1974) *Governing the University*. San Francisco: Jossey Bass.

Estermann, T, Nokakala, T, and Steinal, M (2011) *University Autonomy in Europe II*. Brussels: European Universities Association.

European Commission (2016) *Peer Review of the Hungarian Research and Innovation System*. Brussels: European Commission.

European Universities Association (2017) *University Autonomy in Europe III*. Brussels: European Universities Association.

European Universities Association (2020) *EUA Public Funding Observatory Report 2019/2020*. Brussels: European Universities Association.

Hazelkorn, E (2015) *Rankings and the Reshaping of Higher Education: The Battle for World Class Excellence* (2nd edition). Dordrecht: Springer.

Jessop, B (2008) 'A cultural political economy of competitiveness and its implications for higher education'. In Jessop, B, Fairclough, N and Wodack, R (Eds.), *Education and the Knowledge Based Economy in Europe*. Rotterdam: Sense Publishers, 11–39.

Klemenčič, M (2012) 'The changing conception of student participation in higher education governance in the European Higher Education Area'. In Curaj, A, Scott, P, Vlasceanu, L, and Wilson, L (Eds.), *European Higher Education at the Crossroads: Between the Bologna Process and National Reforms*. Dordrecht: Springer, 631–53.

Kovatz, G, Weston, B, and Chandler, N (2017) 'The pendulum strikes back? An analysis of Hungarian higher education governance and organization structures since the 1980s'. *European Educational Research Journal* 16(5), 568–87.

Kruger, K, Parallada, M, Samoilivich, D, and Sursock, A (2018) *Governance Reforms in European Systems: The Case of Austria, Denmark, Finland, France, the Netherlands and Portugal*. Dordrecht: Springer.

Loveday, V (2018) 'The neurotic academic: Anxiety, casualization and governance in the neoliberalising university'. *Journal of Cultural Economy* 11(2), 154–66. DOI:10.1080/17530350.2018.1426032.

Moodie, G and Eustace, R B (1974) *Power and Authority in British Universities*. London: Allen and Unwin.

Musselin, C (2004) 'Towards a European academic labour market? Some lessons drawn from empirical studies on academic mobility'. *Higher Education* 48, 55–78.

Musselin, C and Texeira, P N (2014) 'Introduction'. In Musselin, C and Texeira, P N (Eds.), *Reforming Higher Education. Public Policy Design and Implementation* (Higher Education Dynamics Vol 41). Dordrecht: Springer, 1–20.

Neave, G and Amaral, J (Eds.) (2012) *Higher Education in Portugal 1974–2009*. Dordrecht: Springer.

Nielsen, G B (2015) *Figuration Work: Student Participation, Democracy and University Reform in a Global Knowledge Economy.* Vol 27. Berghahn Books: The EASA Series.

Olsen, J P (2007) 'The institutional dynamics of the European university'. In Maasen, P and Olsen, J P (Eds.), *University Dynamics and European Integration* (Higher Education Dynamics Vol 19). Dordrecht: Springer, 25–54.

Orban, V. (2021) Direct quote from the interview in Radio Kossuth's Good Morning, Hungary! program on 30 April 2021 (from minutes 17.33 to 17.37). Retrieved on 3 May 2022 from https://mediaklikk.hu/miniszterelnoki-interjuk/cikk/2021/04/30/orban-viktor-miniszterelnoki-interju-jo-reggelt-magyarorszag-aprilis-30/.

Paradeise, C, Reale, E, Bleike, I, Ferlie, E (2009) *University Governance Western European Perspectives.* Dordrecht: Springer.

Park, E (2013) 'From academic self governance to executive university management: Institutional governance in the eyes of academics in Europe'. In *The Work Situation of the Academic Profession in Europe: Findings of a Survey in twelve Countries.* Dordrecht: Springer, 183–203. The Changing Academy – The Changing Academic Profession in International Comparative Perspective. Web.

OECD (2017) *Education at a Glance 2017.* Paris: OECD.

Riddell, S, Weston, E, and Minty, S (Eds.) (2016) *Higher Education in Scotland and the UK. Diverging or Converging Systems.* Edinburgh: Edinburgh Press.

Robinson, E (1968) *The New Polytechnics.* London: Cornmarket.

Rowlands, J (2019) 'The domestic labour of academic governance and the loss of academic voice'. *Gender and Education* 31(7), 793–810. DOI:10.1080/09540253.2017.1324132.

Ruegg, W (Ed.) (2004) *A History of the University in Europe Vol III.* Cambridge: Cambridge University Press.

Scottish Government (2007) *Principles and Priorities: The Government's Programme for Scotland.* Edinburgh: Scottish Government.

Shattock, M L (2006) *Managing Good Governance in Higher Education.* Maidenhead: Open University Press.

Shattock, M L (Ed.) (2014) *International Trends in University Governance.* Abingdon: Routledge.

Shattock, M L (2016) 'The financing of British higher education: The triumph of process over policy'. In Barnett, R, Temple, P and Scott, P (Eds.), *Valuing Higher Education.* London: UCL IoE Press, 59–76.

Shattock, M L, and Horvath, A (2019) *The Governance of British Higher Education: The Impact of Governmental, Financial and Market Pressures.* London: Bloomsbury.

Teichler, U (2018) 'Germany: Continuous intergovermental negotiations'. In Carnoy, M, Froumin, I, Leshukov, O, and Marginson, S (Eds.), *Higher Education in Federal Countries: A Comparative Study*. Dordrecht: Springer, 173–211.

Vernon, K (2004) *Universities and the State in England 1850-1939*. Abingdon: Routledge.

Voegtle, E M, Knill, C, and Dobson, M (2011) 'To what extent does transnational communication drive cross-national policy convergence? The impact of the Bologna Process on domestic higher education policies'. *Higher Education* 61(1), 77–94.

Weber, M (1968 [1917]) 'Wissenschaft als Beruf'. In *Max Weber: Gesammelte Aufsatze zur Wissenschaftslehere* (3.Auflage). Tubingen: Mohr, 582–613.

Whitley, R and Glaser, J (2014) 'The impact of institutional reforms on the nature of universities as organizations'. *Research in the Sociology of Organizations* 42, 19–49.

Willetts, D (2017) *A University Education*. Oxford: Oxford University Press.

Index

Aberdeen, Scottish Ancient Universities 12, 32
academic(s)
   decision-making 6, 18, 38, 84, 97, 113, 166
   freedom 11–12, 17
   labour market 144
   mobility 143
   oligarchy 84
   restrictions 181
academic accountability 43–4, 76, 83, 86, 94, 103, 156, 164
academic community 6, 19–21, 38, 52, 76, 80–3, 97–8, 101, 104, 127, 179
   in continental universities 180
   England 52, 113, 137–8
   against external intervention 110
   fluctuations 137
   Germany 88
   and governance of teaching 144–53
   Hungary 6, 97–8
   job-hopping 137
   and management 93
   Norway 93
   Portugal 101
   in senior executive positions 138–44
accountability 15, 28, 43–4, 76, 83, 86, 94, 103, 143, 156, 164, 177
Agency for Assessment and Accreditation of Higher Education (Portugal) 144–5, 149
Aghion, P 19, 83, 179
Agricultural University (Hungary) 68
Alises Nationales de l'Enseignement Supérieur et de la Recherche 15
Amaral, A 15, 40
American universities 82, 172
anchor institution 61, 67, 99
Anglophone model 4–5, 9–14, 17, 45–6, 79–81, 83, 105, 111, 166, 175
Association of Arctic Universities 66

autonomization 84
autonomy 7, 9, 12, 20, 27–8, 40–1, 51, 69, 87, 92–3, 95, 97–8, 102, 162
   academic and financial 13, 21, 38, 53, 80, 100, 181
   and accountability 156
   classroom 147–8, 151
   decision-making 156
   of faculties 6, 92–3, 113, 127
   institutional 5, 10–11, 14, 18, 33–5, 38, 42, 44–6, 97–8, 107, 127, 179
   legal and substantive 13, 40, 41, 45, 167
   operational 11, 14, 17, 41, 45, 167
   operational freedom and 111
   self-government 28
Autonomy Scorecards (EUA, 2011) 13

Bell, D 175
Bergen, universities 29, 63, 73, 90, 108
binary lines/systems 5, 56–60, 72, 182
   Germany 59–60, 75
   Norway 90
   Portugal 60
   regional factors in diversification 60–6
   reshaping 67–70
   second-tier institutions 59–60
   UK 58, 67
Bird, R 105
Blackmore, J 137
Blair, T 50
Bleiklie, I 3, 162
block grant funding system 15, 22, 84, 129, 130–1, 133
Bologna Declaration (1999) 1
Bologna Process 1, 4–5, 19, 43, 55, 69, 79, 145, 177, 184
box-ticking game 124, 136
Braganza 61
Brexit Referendum 32
Brooks, R 114
Budapest University of Economics 68

budgets 20, 22, 29, 33, 42, 50, 65, 81, 86–7, 94, 127–8, 130–1, 135, 183
　decision-making 18
　diversifying 106
　faculty 92, 94, 100
　Germany 23
　HAC 145
　management 100
　students organizations and funding 128–32
bureaucracy 9–10, 38, 40–2, 46, 99, 102, 164, 166
business model of university governance 44, 69, 85, 91–2, 96, 103

Cambridge University 25, 80, 103, 108, 179–80
Cardiff Metropolitan University 31, 65, 108
Cardoso, A H 15
Carnoy, M 3
Central European University 17, 177
Centre National de la Recherche Scientifique (CRNS) (France) 10, 80
the chancellor/chancellor system (Hungary) 17, 37–9, 46, 69, 76, 84, 86, 95–8, 108–9, 150, 177, 181
Chandler, N 35
Chartelain-Ponroy, S 3, 10, 15
CHEPS 3
Clark, B R 84
classroom autonomy 147–8, 151
Coimbra University 39, 61
College of Pedagogy (Hungary) 72
College of Public Administration (Hungary) 68
Colleges of Advanced Technology (CATs) (UK) 57–8
Commission of the European Communities (CEC) 83
Committee of University Chairs (CUC) 103
Committee of Vice-Chancellors and Principals (CVCP) 27
Committee on Higher Education, Report 57
competition and choice policy 26
Conference of University Rectors (Germany) 20

Conference of University Rectors (Portugal) 40
continental university 6–7, 12, 110, 113, 137–44, 179–80, 183
convergence and divergence 4, 7–8, 107, 110–11, 156, 160, 171–3, 177–8, 180–4
　academic staff participation 180
　funding agenda 183
　institutional management 179, 181
　Norway 178
　Wales 178
corporate actor, university as 7, 162–4, 166, 174
Corvinus University 68–9, 95–6
Council for National Academic Awards (CNAA) (UK) 57–8

Dearing Report 82
De Boer, H 3, 9, 163, 171
decision-making 6, 18, 21, 36, 38, 50, 59–60, 76–7, 84, 87–8, 97, 102, 109, 113
　academic 97, 113, 166
　autonomy 156
　Bavaria 84
　culture and 183
　Germany 18, 92, 94, 178
　Hungary 6, 50
　institutional 92, 107
　key management 180
　Portugal 125
　power 21, 27
　state 111
　UK 6–7, 113, 124
de-contextualization, universities 171
de-coupling funding 158
demystification process 7, 173
Department for Business, Energy and Industrial Strategy (BEIS, UK) 24–5, 47
Department for Business, Innovation and Skills (BIS, UK) 24, 26
Department for Education (DfE, UK) 24–5, 47
Department of Education and Science (DES, UK) 24
Department of Innovation, Universities and Skills (DIU, UK) 24

Department of Trade and Industry (DTI, UK) 24
Deprecen 62
Deutsche Forschungsgemeinschaft (DFG, Germany) 20, 23, 80, 88
devolution 16, 24, 64, 169
direct state funding systems 105–7
diversification/diversity 2, 5, 16, 55
   in European systems 74–7
   institutional governance 107
   institutions and in system architectures 70–4
   regional factors 60–6
   and stratification 168
   unity and 170
Dobson, M 19

East German system 16
Economic and Social Research Council (ESRC, UK) 1
Edinburgh, Scottish Ancient University 12, 32–4, 66, 108
Enders, J 2–3, 8–9, 138, 162–3, 171–2
England (UK) 2, 8, 29–30, 44, 55–7, 61, 66, 76, 79, 161, 177–8, 182–3
   academic mobility 143
   academics/academic community 52, 113, 137–8
   alternative patterns of development 102–5
   decentralization of higher education 64
   decision-making 6–7, 113, 124
   English system as a market 26
   funding 13, 45, 81, 105–7, 129
   governance, historic patterns of 15
   governing bodies 102–4, 121
   higher education 58, 67
   institutional restructuring effect 59
   lay involvement 6, 179
   marketization 33, 52, 106–7, 151, 183
   modernization 24–7
   national-level student leader 119–20
   policy development 57
   polytechnics 69
   powers 142
   REF 83
   research and education 49
   student participation/accommodation 114, 118, 123–4, 132, 135
   Student Unions 115
   subject communities 148
   teaching and learning forum 148
   unified system 182
   Universities UK (UUK) 52
   university-state relations 80–1
entrepreneurial university 163
Eötvös Loránd University (ELTE) 17, 36, 44, 62, 65, 68, 73–4, 93–4, 108
Epstein, L D 179
Estermann, T 13
EU Declaration (2000) 48
EU Horizon programme 1, 79
European Association for Quality Assurance (ENQA) 40
European Commission 49
European Higher Education Area 1, 170–1, 184
European Student Union (ESU) 120
European systems, diversity 74–7
   research dimension 76
   second-tier institutions 75–6
   size 74–5
European Universities Association (EUA) 13, 36, 43
Eustace, R B 27
executive teams/the executive 6, 15, 21–3, 81–2, 88, 92–3, 102–4, 107, 109–10, 113, 123–5, 127, 133, 137–42, 149, 164, 179–80
external (lay) members 6, 12, 27–8, 42, 44, 84–5, 88, 90–2, 94, 97–8, 101–2, 108–10, 139, 165, 179
Exzellenzinitiative 16, 23–4, 45, 47, 59, 83, 109

Fachhochschulen 5, 47, 57–8, 60–1, 67, 75–6, 90, 182
faculties 6, 10, 18, 21, 37, 62, 71–2, 83–4, 86–7, 91–7, 100–1, 105–6, 110, 113, 119, 126–8, 131, 137–42, 145, 147–50, 180–1
Federal Ministry of Education and Research 20
Federal Ministry of the Exzellenzinitiative 16
Ferlie, E 3
Fidesz 35
File, J 3

financial accountability 43–4, 76, 83, 86, 94, 177
France 3–4, 10, 18, 44, 55–9, 73, 168, 182
   CRNS 80
   education and research 48
   fragmented system, rationalization 75
   governance, historic patterns of 15
   grandes ecoles 172
   legislations 161
   Napoleonic tradition 14
   research evaluation exercises 73
   research funding 172
Frauhofer Gesellschaft 23, 47, 80
Free Association of Student Bodies (Germany) 115, 120
Froumin, I 3

German Research Council (Berlin) 47
Germany 2–3, 44–5, 55–6, 63, 67, 80, 90, 92, 101–3, 106–7, 121, 132, 141, 168, 172, 182. *See also* Länder (Germany)
   binary line 59–60
   budgets, universities 23
   control and management 26
   decision-making 18, 92, 94, 178
   devolution 16
   distributed excellence 83, 108
   education and research 47–8
   expansion of student numbers 74
   external national-level accreditation processes 146
   Exzellenzinitiative 25, 45
   Free Association of Student Bodies 115
   governance model 88–9, 180
   homogeneous living conditions principle 28
   Humboldtian university system 16
   institutional distribution 60
   modernization 19–23, 93
   parliaments, student 115–16
   professional academic leadership 140
   research evaluation exercises 73, 75
   steering higher education 161
   student representative 118
   student welfare issues 135
   teaching, governance of 153
   technical university, academic 147
   universities and state governments 50
   university-state relations 83–9
Gläser, J 167
Glasgow, Scottish Ancient Universities 12, 32, 66, 108
Governance Reforms in European University Systems: The Case of Austria, Denmark, Finland, France, the Netherlands and Portugal (Kruger, Parallada, Samoilivich, & Sursock) 3
governing bodies 6, 12, 18, 27, 30, 33–4, 46, 51, 68, 81–2, 102–4, 108, 110, 120, 122, 133, 177, 180
governmental funding 161, 164–5
grandes écoles 14, 172
Guild HE 72

Hazelkorn, E 171
Heldrich, B 35
Higher Education and Research Act (2017) (UK) 45
Higher Education Code of Governance (UK) 103
Higher Education Funding Council for England (HEFCE) 14, 24–5, 45, 50, 107–8
Higher Education Funding Council for Wales (HEFCW). *See* Tertiary Education and Research Commission (Wales)
Higher Education Guideline Act (Portugal) 15
Higher Education in Federal Countries: A Comparative Study 3
higher education systems 2, 7, 15, 19, 30–2, 35, 40, 43–4, 46, 50, 56–7, 59–60, 82, 90, 155, 159, 178, 182
   integration and differentiation 72, 79, 159, 167–72, 184
   and labour market 158–60
   modernization (*see* modernization)
   second-tier 59–60, 63, 65, 68, 70, 73–5, 182
   state and 159–62
   state controls 76
   unitary 35, 58–60, 65, 67, 70
hinterland issue 8, 62, 75, 181

Hollande, M 15
Horvath, A 1–2, 8, 14, 26, 32, 34, 45, 103–5, 109, 166
   The Governance of British Higher Education 109
   university governance, laicisation 103
Humboldt, W von 11
Humboldtian model 2–5, 9–13, 16–18, 28, 35, 46, 80, 89, 93, 98, 161, 168, 175
Humboldt University 10–11, 16
Hungarian Academy of Sciences 16, 49
Hungarian Accreditation Committee (HAC) 145–6, 149
Hungary 2–3, 44–6, 49, 55, 62, 93, 102, 161, 168, 177–8, 180–1
   academic community 6, 97–8
   academic programmes 149
   accreditation 7, 53
   administrative-professional staff 142
   budget, student council's 115, 130
   chancellors/chancellor system 46, 76, 150, 181
   classic Humboldt-style structure 18
   classroom autonomy and freedom 151
   competing interests 124–5
   Constitution 35
   decision-making 6, 50
   elite universities 73
   external accreditation 7
   funding 105
   governance 39
   interventionist approach 107
   merger policy 65
   modernization 35–9, 98, 177
   neo-liberal system 35
   political parties 118
   political vicissitudes 16
   polytechnics 59
   post-binary system 71
   regional factors in system diversification 62, 64
   Student Councils 115
   student participation 118–19, 122, 124–5, 132
   student unions 124
   student welfare issues 134
   universities and government 11, 51
   university-state relations 93–9

Illyes Gyula College (Szekszard) 72
'The Impact of Recent Reforms in the Institutional Governance of French Universities' (Chartelain-Ponroy, Mignot-Gerard, Musselin, & Sporiam) 3
Initiative d'Excellence (IDEX) (France) 14, 24, 48
institutional autonomy 5, 10–11, 14, 18, 33–5, 38, 42, 44–6, 97–8, 107, 127, 179
institutional competition 83, 89
institutional governance 22, 31, 69, 79, 99, 139, 169, 178, 180–1
   changes 9
   convergence and divergence 7–8
   diversity 107
   division of 84
   external (lay) membership 8, 27, 44, 179–80
   funding mechanisms and 105–7
   impact 76, 83, 99–100
   implications 27
   laicisation 103
   modernization 6
   structures 79, 93, 96, 100, 102
   student inclusion and weight 136–7
   and system reform 107–11
   within universities, changing participation 6–7
institutional management 18, 21, 42, 76, 109, 179
institutional rankings 5, 15, 19, 34, 58, 72–4, 168, 171–2
Instituts Universitaires de Technologie (IUTs) (France) 58
intermediary bodies 8, 13–14, 31, 33, 45, 50, 66, 107, 111, 178
international organizations 171
Isle of Skye 66
Italy 3–4, 14, 44, 48, 77, 182
   governance 15
   legislations 161
   Napoleonic rule 10, 14
   research evaluation exercises 73

Janus Pannonius University 72
Jarratt Report 27, 82
Jessop, B 159

joint university research centres 41, 62, 70, 72
Jongblood, B 3

Kanzler 11, 20, 84–5, 88, 95
Kings and University Colleges 108
Klemenčič, M 114
Knill, C 19
knowledge society 155, 159–60, 172–3
Kovatz, G 35, 68
Kruger, K 3

Labour Student's Society (UK) 118
Länder (Germany) 11, 16, 20–2, 45, 47, 52, 85, 87, 93, 121, 169, 178–80
 devolution 16, 47, 169
 funding 23, 84
 Higher Education Pact 23
 homogeneity 60, 63, 108
 management-orientated 22
 micro-management 21
 negotiation 22, 89
 system governance 23
Lapori, B 3
The Law on the Freedom of Universities (*Hochschulfreiheitsgesezt*) 20
Leibnitz Association 23, 47
Leisyte, L 163
Lepori, B 162
Leshukov, O 3
Libertés et Responsabilités des Universités (France) 14
Lisbon Academic Federation 115
Lisbon Declaration 19, 184
Lisbon universities 39, 41, 44, 61–2, 73–5, 108
Loi pour la recherche et l'innovation (LOPRI) (France) 14, 48
London School of Economics 108
Loveday, V 137

manager-academics 138–44
Managing Universities, Policy and Organizational Change from a Western European Perspective (Bleiklie, Enders, & Lapori) 3
Marginson, S 3
marketization 27, 33, 52, 106–7, 138, 151, 183

massification 5, 7–8, 43, 55, 59–60, 79, 82, 157, 181, 183
 and austerity 177
 and modernization 155
Max Planck Society 23, 47, 80
mergers, institutional 5, 28–31, 35, 44–5, 57, 60, 65–9, 71, 75, 161
Mertonian process 73
Mignot-Gerard, S 3
Million Plus (UK) 72
Ministry of Education and Research (Norway) 27, 90
Ministry of Education and Science (Portugal) 41
Minty, S 32
mission overload 173
modernization 17, 19, 43, 83, 93, 109, 155, 159, 162, 165, 167, 172, 177–8, 184
 decision-making structures 6
 England 24–7
 Germany 19–23, 93
 growth and 157–9
 higher education revisited 172–5
 historic patterns, strategies 14–19
 Hungary 35–9, 98, 177
 institutional governance 6
 Norway 27–9, 93
 Portugal 39–42
 Scotland 32–5
 Wales 29–31
mono-disciplinary institutions 68
Moodie, G 27
Moscati, R 3, 15
Musselin, C 3, 15, 144, 158

Napoleonic model 3–5, 9–14, 17–18, 80, 161, 175
National Committee of Student Unions (NCSU) (Hungary) 119
National Foundation for Science and Technology (NFST) (Portugal) 41, 48–9, 102
National Research, Development and Innovation Office (NRDIO) (Hungary) 49
National Research Agency (ANR) France) 48
National Student Survey (NSS) (UK) 119, 129

National Union of Students (NUS) (UK) 115, 119–20
Neave, G 15, 40
New Public Management 82, 157, 159–60, 163, 174, 178
Nielsen, G B 114
non-university institutions 56, 60, 67, 168
Nordic welfare state 28, 64
Norway 2–3, 30–1, 44–5, 52–3, 63–4, 74–5, 103, 106, 108–9, 161, 168, 178, 180–2
  academics 139–40, 152
  administrative-professional staff 142
  Centre Party 64
  competing interests 125
  decentralized system deans 92
  divergence 178
  education and research 48
  external national-level accreditation processes 146–7
  faculty budgets 92
  financial punishments 130
  financial sustainability 68
  funding 29, 36, 130
  governance 51, 122
  higher education policy 63–4
  managing student welfare issues 133
  market demand 152
  merger policy 65
  modernization 27–9, 93
  NOKUT 53
  political parties 117
  professional academic leadership 140–1
  Quality Reform 27, 29, 45, 64, 71, 89–90
  rector and board 127
  regional politics 28
  student administration/officers 123, 132
  Student Parliament 115–17, 126, 133–4
  student unions 123
  student welfare organizations 114–15, 120, 124, 126, 133–4
  unitary higher education system 60
  university-state relations 12, 89–93
Norwegian Agency for Quality Assurance in Education (NOKUT) 27–9, 53, 68, 71, 90, 147

Norwegian Labour Party 117
Norwegian Research Council (RCN) 29

Office for Students (OfS) (UK) 14, 25, 107–8, 119, 121, 179
operational activities 95
Orban, V 38
Organisation for Economic Cooperation and Development (OECD) 42, 63, 94, 171
Orkneys 66
Oslo, universities 29, 44, 63, 71, 73–4, 90, 108
Outer Hebrides 66
Oxford University 25, 80, 103, 108, 179–80

Paradeise, C 3
Parallada, M 3
Park, E 137
Pécs University 62, 65, 71–3
'the People's Universities' (UK) 57
performance-based funding systems 158
Pôle de recherche et d'enseignement supérieur (PRES) (France) 14
policymaking, institutional 87, 93–4, 103, 105–6, 153, 160, 170
  autonomization 84
  diversity 160
  national-level 136–7
  variation in 161, 174
polytechnics 5, 32, 39, 47–8, 57–61, 63, 69, 70, 72, 74, 99–100
  en bloc 182
  merging 61
  UK 69–70, 75, 102
Porto University 39, 41, 44, 61–2, 73–5, 108
Porto Academic Federation 115
Portugal 2–3, 16, 19, 45–6, 55, 61–4, 69, 72–6, 93, 103, 105–10, 117, 124–8, 132, 135, 149–50, 168, 177, 181–2
  academic community and deans 142
  Academic Federation for Information and External Representation 115
  academic programmes 149
  accreditation 7, 53
  administrative-professional staff 142
  binary line 60
  budgetary concerns 128, 131

decision-making 124
education and research 48–9
external accreditation 7
funding 105
governance of teaching 144–5
inter-institutional activity 72
Lisbon Academic Federation 115
modernization 39–42
Napoleonic rule 10
NFST 41, 48–9, 102
polytechnics 59
Porto Academic Federation 115
regional factors in system
    diversification 64
reliance on state control 15
research and teaching 127
Salazar dictatorship 99
state reforms 161
Student Associations 115
student federations 117
student unions 131
student welfare issues 135–6
university governing bodies 120
university-state relations 99–102
professional academic leadership 140
    Germany 141
    Norway 141–2
Progress in Higher Education Reform in Europe Part I Governance Reform (de Boer, Jongblood, Enders, & File) 3
Prussian university system 88

Quality Assurance Agency (QAA) (UK) 32, 53, 67, 148
Quality Research (QR) (UK) 24
quasi-independent research centres (Portugal) 41, 102

raison d'être of university councils 85
R&D 19, 48–9
Reale, E 3
rectors and deans 6, 13, 17–18, 37–9, 41, 50–2, 79–80, 82–3, 86–7, 92–4, 100, 104, 109–10, 137, 142–3, 145, 165, 174, 179–80
regional colleges/university 5, 7, 71, 90, 116, 142, 150, 168–9
regional demographies 61–2

regional disparities 5, 61, 161
Research Assessment Exercise (RAE). *See* Research Excellence Framework (REF)
Research Excellence Framework (REF) (UK) 24, 34, 47, 58, 83
research-intensive universities 25, 28, 34, 59, 72–3, 75, 111, 143, 165, 171, 180
research university 41, 63, 68, 73, 80, 86, 142–3, 146–8, 152, 166, 168, 171
    France 172
    Germany 108–9
    Hungary 118, 150
    Norway 63, 68, 139, 147
    Portugal 142
    UK 148
Revolution (1974–6) (Portugal) 15
Riddell, S 32
Robbins Committee 57
Robinson, E 58
Rowlands, J 137
Ruegg, W 11, 80
Russell Group university 25, 31, 34, 66, 72, 143

Salazar dictatorship/regime 15, 39–40, 42, 99
Salmond, A 32
Samoilivich, D 3
Schleiermacher, F 11
Scotland 2, 24–5, 29, 50, 52, 57, 64–6, 70, 74, 79, 107–8, 135, 177, 182–3
    alternative patterns of development 102–5
    Ancient Universities 12, 80
    fee-paid approach 183
    higher education systems 64–5
    modernization 32–5
    student accommodation 135
    universities and government 33, 66
Scottish Central Institutions 32, 47, 57–8, 61, 65, 70, 75
Scottish Funding Council (SFC) 14, 33, 52, 66
Scottish National Enterprise Board 33
Scottish National Party (SNP) 32–3, 45–6, 66
second-tier institutions 59–60, 63, 65, 68, 70, 73–5, 182

senates and academic boards 6, 10, 18, 21–3, 27, 35, 37–8, 81–2, 87, 90, 94, 100, 101–2, 104, 113, 122–4, 133, 138, 165–6, 179–81
Shanghai Jiao Tong World University ranking 19, 41
shared governance 18, 82, 136
Shattock, M L 1–3, 8, 13–14, 25–6, 32, 34, 45, 82, 103–5, 109, 166
  The Governance of British Higher Education 109
  International Trends in University Governance 3
  university governance, laicisation 103
Socialist Worker Society 118
Sorbonne Declaration (1998) 1
South Eastern University 71
Sporiam, S 3
Standing Conference of the Ministers of Education and Culture (Germany) 20
St Andrews, Scottish Ancient Universities 12, 32
states and institutions 5, 9, 63, 69, 76, 129, 133, 136, 156–7, 164, 174, 178, 183
  alternative patterns of development 80–105
  changing role 43–4
  expansion 43–4
  and higher education landscape 159–62
  institutional autonomy 45–6
  marketization 151
  politico-administrative structure 169
  and public service organizations 157
  reforms (Portugal) 161
  research from teaching 46–49
  scholarship system 73
  system management 50–2
  trust 52–3
  vis-à-vis 107, 109, 173
state steering 17, 45, 76–7, 111, 178
the student body 7, 87, 113, 115–16, 118, 125–7, 136, 181
students in university governance 114, 181
  at faculties and departments 126–8
  inclusion and weight 136–7
  on institutional policy 121–6
  at national and regional levels 115–21

organizations and their funding 115, 128–32
  participation 113
  student welfare issues, organizations 132–6
supervisory model 15, 40, 161
supreme academic authority 81
Sursock, A 3
system governance/management 5–7, 46, 50–2, 55, 76, 89, 107, 169, 177, 182
  intervention 178
  new approaches 178
Szeged University 73

teaching and research 9, 11–12, 25, 46–9, 84, 86, 88, 102, 104, 153, 167, 172, 175, 183
  commodification 164
  de-coupling funding 158
  integration 49, 161, 182
  Napoleonic approach 161
  quality of 138
Teaching Excellence Framework 118
teaching only university 32, 58, 182
Technical College in Pécs 72
Teichler, U 3, 16, 20–1, 89
  Germany: Continuous Intergovernmental Negotiations 3
Tertiary Education and Research Commission (Wales) 14, 31
tertiary education system 31, 66, 177
Texeira, P N 158
third party funding 86, 89
traditional steering model 9
Tromsoe University 63
Trondheim University 63, 73, 90, 108
tuition fees 18, 23, 25, 29–31, 34, 36, 42–3, 50, 81, 83, 106, 119, 165, 177, 183
two-tier systems 5, 93

UNESCO 171
unitary higher education 35, 58–60, 65, 67, 70
United States
  institution-based research excellence 89
  state university systems 74
  universities 82, 98, 110, 171–2, 179

universities of applied science 5, 39, 60, 63–4, 76, 90–1, 99, 158, 182
Universities Scotland 33–4, 66
universities/university system 1–3, 19, 28, 37, 44, 56–7, 63, 75, 98, 182. *See also specific universities*
    as an organization 156–7, 162–7, 174
    changing idea and role 7
    as corporate actor 162–3, 166–7, 174
    as cultural institution 156, 173
    de-contextualization 171
    diversity (*see* diversification/diversity)
    and government 12, 33, 50–1
    mission groups 169
    pre- and post-1992 58–9, 66–7, 70, 72–3, 103–4
    reshaping 14, 172
    roles and development 155–6
University Governance Western European Perspectives (Paradeise, Reale, Bleiklie, & Ferlie) 3
University Grants Committee (UGC) (UK) 13–14, 18, 24, 57, 82, 107
University of California, Berkeley 95
University of South Wales 65
University of the Highlands and Islands (Scotland) 33, 66
University of Trás os Montes e Alto Douro (UTAD) 69–70
University of Wales 30
university-state relations 12, 50–1, 68, 80, 178, 183
    Germany 83–9

Hungary 93–9
Norway 89–93
UK 80–1

Vernon, K 81
Vila Real Polytechnic Institute 69–70
vocational/technological institutions 57–8, 60, 69
Voegtle, E M 19

Wales/Welsh 2, 24, 34, 50, 66, 70, 74–5, 79, 108, 177–8
    alternative patterns of development 102–5
    Assembly Labour Government policy 30
    divergence 178
    economy 30
    higher education systems 64–5
    institutions and government 30–1
    modernization 29–31
    overprovision 65
    post-devolution 30
    universities 12, 30–1
Weber, M 173
Weston, E 32
Whitley, R 167
Willetts, D 26. *See also* competition and choice policy
Wissenschaftsrat (Science Council) 20
World Bank 171
world-class university 7, 161, 168, 171–2, 174–5

www.ingramcontent.com/pod-product-compliance
Lightning Source LLC
Chambersburg PA
CBHW062227300426
44115CB00012BA/2250